Uncommonly Corduroy

QUILT PATTERNS, BAG PATTERNS, AND MORE

Stephanie Dunphy

Martingale
Create with Confidence

Dedication

In memory of my friend Linda Lascola, who is undoubtedly appliquéing the most heavenly quilts.

Uncommonly Corduroy:
Quilt Patterns, Bag Patterns, and More
© 2014 by Stephanie Dunphy

Martingale®
19021 120th Ave. NE, Ste. 102
Bothell, WA 98011-9511 USA
ShopMartingale.com

Printed in China
19 18 17 16 15 14   8 7 6 5 4 3 2 1

Library of Congress Cataloging-in-Publication Data is available upon request.

ISBN: 978-1-60468-399-8

Mission Statement
Dedicated to providing quality products and service to inspire creativity.

CREDITS

PRESIDENT AND CEO: Tom Wierzbicki

EDITOR IN CHIEF: Mary V. Green

DESIGN DIRECTOR: Paula Schlosser

MANAGING EDITOR: Karen Costello Soltys

ACQUISITIONS EDITOR: Karen M. Burns

TECHNICAL EDITOR: Nancy Mahoney

COPY EDITOR: Melissa Bryan

PRODUCTION MANAGER: Regina Girard

COVER AND INTERIOR DESIGNER: Adrienne Smitke

PHOTOGRAPHER: Brent Kane

ILLUSTRATOR: Missy Shepler

Special thanks to Cliff and Rosemary Bailey of Snohomish, Washington, for generously allowing us to photograph at their home.

CONTENTS

ODE TO CORDUROY

My twist on *'Twas the Night Before Christmas*
by Clement Clarke Moore.

Ode to Corduroy

'Twas the early 1970s
When I was in school
Wearing corduroy hip huggers
Bell bottoms were cool.

As the decades passed by
Corduroy seemed to fade
Now it's back in style
In most every shade.

With the velvety goodness
Of prints and solids galore
Quilt-fabric designers
Have me eager for more.

One day I created
A corduroy tote
Shared my excitement with my son,
His interest was remote.

With a turn of his head
And a quizzical glance
I heard him reply,
"Corduroy is for pants!"

I've created some projects
Using velvety corduroy
Bags, quilts, and a scarf
For you to enjoy.

Whether you're new to these crafts
Or passed down through generations
It's my forever hope
You enjoy your creations!

~Piecefully,
Stephanie

GETTING STARTED

Thank goodness for corduroy pants!

Before you begin your projects—especially if you're planning to use corduroy for the first time—I suggest you look over the following information to help you achieve success.

TIPS FOR SUCCESS

Although I don't always take my own advice, I hope the tips in this section help you avoid spending too much time with your seam ripper.

* Read all directions before beginning each project.
* Measure twice, cut once.
* Make a sample block before cutting the fabric for the entire quilt. (I like to do this to check my measurements and verify that I've cut the corduroy nap correctly.) Perhaps you can incorporate your sample block into the quilt back if you don't want to use it on the quilt top.

TERMINOLOGY

These handy dandy terms and tips are for your general reference. Use them as a guide and do what works best for you. When your machine speaks, listen.

Corduroy. Corduroy is available in 100% cotton and also cotton/spandex blends. All corduroy used in this book is 100% cotton. The stretchy type is great for clothing, but not good for quilting.

Nap. Corduroy has a nap and is a very tactile fabric. When you pet it in one direction it's soft and velvety, but run your hand in the other direction and it's rough and bumpy.

For clothing and furniture upholstery, it's best to have the nap going in one direction so that you don't make "seat" prints. However, with quilts and bags the consistency or direction of the nap is less important. To keep the nap in one direction often requires extra yardage and is noted in the project's instructions, when applicable.

Wale. When purchasing corduroy, you will often encounter a number that refers to the size of the wale (the number of ridges per inch). The lower the number, the wider the wale (4-wale corduroy has a much wider wale than 21-wale), and the size of the wale can vary considerably. Usually the wale and nap run the length of the fabric.

Most of the corduroy I use is the 21-wale variety. It's light, drapey-soft, and easy to work with, making it perfect for quilts as well as bags. For bag projects that need to be especially sturdy, however, wider-wale corduroy is a good choice.

Pressing. To keep the nap smooth and velvety, you'll want to press in the direction of the nap. Both steam pressing and dry pressing have strong supporters. I'm a steam girl and I prefer to press on the right side. You don't need to use a pressing cloth, unless you want to.

Luscious corduroy for cozy creations

Width of fabric. Corduroy comes in varying widths. *All* yardage requirements and cutting directions in this book are based on 42" of usable fabric. That way the yardage is consistent if you wish to make your projects using the familiar quilting cottons instead of corduroy.

Sewing machine. My machine is good to me, and I repay the favor by keeping her clean between projects and taking her to be professionally cleaned and serviced once a year. Corduroy and flannel create a lot of lint fuzzies.

Needles. I keep a stock of universal 80/12 and 90/14 needles handy. Changing needles often helps keep a smooth stitch. I find that 90/14 needles "get the job done" when working with the bulk of heavier fabrics and stabilizers.

Thread. I use cotton threads or cotton/polyester blends. Your machine will tell you what thread it likes best. I keep an array of colors handy, especially for machine quilting my bags.

Lint roller. When cutting corduroy, you'll create corduroy dust. I keep a lint roller handy not only for removing the dust from my clothes but also to remove the threads and other lint that cling to the corduroy.

Prewashing. I prewash all fabrics for a few reasons: to shrink, to set color, and to soften. Corduroy can feel quite stiff before washing. I find it's easier to work with once it's been washed.

Dye or color catchers. I use a dye-catcher sheet when I prewash and also when washing projects after they are constructed, especially those projects using darker colors, to prevent excess dye from staining the lighter fabrics.

Project piles. This is where I gather materials, buttons, and trim for a particular project and let them hang out to see if they want to be friends. I keep the pile visible so that I can take frequent peeks, removing elements that don't appear to play well with others or adding new friends.

BAG-MAKING TIPS

Making a successful bag—one that not only looks nice but is sturdy and keeps its shape—has a lot to do with the products you use for the inside layers of the bag. With such a variety of products available, we all have our favorite brands. I refer to products such as fusible web and stabilizers in general terms, with the exception of Soft and Stable, which is a specific stabilizer product that I use for the majority of my bags. Whatever brand you choose, please be sure to follow the manufacturer's instructions for proper use.

STABILIZERS

Stabilizers give your bags their shape. There are different types and weights of fusible and nonfusible stabilizers.

Soft and Stable. ByAnnie's Soft and Stable (see "Resources" on page 94) is a 100% polyester foam that's firmer than fusible fleece. It is 58" wide on the bolt and also comes prepackaged with four 13½" x 18½" pieces. I use this for almost all of my bag projects because it gives the bags structure, helps them to maintain their shape, and protects against the dreaded saggy-bottom syndrome.

Notice how thick Soft and Stable is compared to the fabric layer.

For best results, cut the stabilizer about 1" larger on all sides than the bag front. Cut a second piece for the bag back in the same manner. Center each bag piece right side up on top of the corresponding piece of Soft and Stable. Smooth your pieces so they lie flat. Pin baste the layers around the edges and in the middle, and then machine quilt as desired. After quilting, machine baste around all four sides before trimming the excess foam even with the bag front and back.

Heavyweight fusible fleece. Sometimes I use a heavyweight fusible fleece as a stabilizer, when I want to reinforce a bag but I also want it to have a soft shape. If you're unable to find Soft and Stable in your area, heavyweight fusible fleece is a good alternative. The brand I use is 47" wide, and the fusible agent is on one side only. Cut the fleece the same size as your bag front and back. Following the product directions, fuse it to the wrong side of your project, and then machine quilt as desired. To add more structure to a bag, fuse a lightweight fleece to the bag's lining pieces. This does make the seam thicker to sew, so be mindful of what your machine can handle.

ADDITIONAL TOOLS AND TECHNIQUES

Have fun, use what you have, and improvise.

Lightweight woven fusible interfacing. Fusible interfacing comes in a variety of weights as well as different material types, including woven, nonwoven, and knit. Look for a lightweight *woven* interfacing. It has a fusible agent on one side and is 20½" wide. I use this for bag handles and also as a stabilizer on the underside of any project that I machine blanket stitch. When called for in the projects, it's optional. However, I like how it keeps bag handles from looking floppy.

Buttons. Buttons make the world go 'round. Buttons are the single most important feature of a bag. They are the finishing touch. That's my story and I'm stickin' to it! Buttons don't have to be expensive, just fantastic. Consider a button from a favorite old

Vintage buttons can add a bit of flair to any bag.

coat, something special from Grandma's button jar, or a new button that catches your eye. I love hunting for vintage buttons.

Rickrack. Does size really matter? The width of rickrack is measured from bump to bump. Use the width called for in these projects as a guideline. The same goes for any other trim. Adding your own special touch is what makes a project your one-of-a-kind creation.

Handles. Speaking of size, pantyhose might be labeled "one size fits all," but that sure doesn't apply to bag handles! Whether you are tall or small, adjusting the bag handle for a comfortable fit is as simple as adding or subtracting length. You can also cut your handle either narrower or wider to suit your taste.

Box-pleated bottom. You may have a favorite way to box-pleat the corners of your bag bottoms, but I'll share the method that works best for me. Each bag pattern indicates the measurement to mark the box pleats for that project.

MAKING BOX-PLEAT CORNERS FOR BAG BOTTOMS

1. With the bag wrong side out, fold one corner of the bag and align the side seam on the bottom seam to form a point.

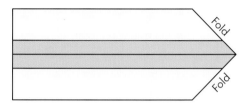

2. On one end, measure the distance specified in the project instructions and draw a line with a ruler.

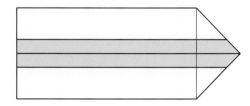

3. Pin to prevent the layers from shifting, and then sew on the drawn line, starting and stopping with a backstitch.

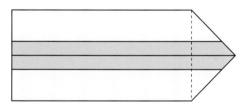

4. Trim the excess stabilizer and fabric ½" beyond the stitched line.

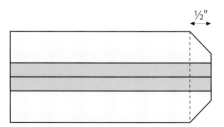

5. Repeat steps 1–4 to box the other corner. Use the same process to box-pleat the bag lining.

QUILTMAKING TIPS

With the multitude of how-to resource books on the market as well as a gazillion online tutorials, I won't cover all the basics of quiltmaking here. Instead, I've pulled together some general tips that work for me, and I hope you will find them helpful as well.

Seam allowance. All of the quilts in this book use a ¼" seam allowance, unless otherwise noted.

Binding. When constructing a quilt using the familiar quilter's cotton fabrics, I cut my binding strips 2½" wide. However, when using heavier-weight fabrics such as corduroy or flannel, I cut the strips 3" wide to allow for the bulk.

Backing. Corduroy makes a wonderful quilt back. I also like to use flannel because of the cozy softness and snuggle factor. Whether you do your own hand or machine quilting or send your quilts out to be professionally quilted, you need extra fabric around the edges. When calculating yardage for quilt backs, I allow 3" to 4" on all sides; therefore, all the backing yardages listed with the projects include an extra 6" to 8" of fabric. I also like to piece quilt backs, getting the maximum use out of fabrics left over from making my quilt tops. When you can use up your fabric leftovers, you might not always need to buy additional fabric for backing. Have fun!

Borders. Accuracy is important in sewing, however it's not my intention to produce show-quality quilts that measure perfectly even on all sides. Most often I cut my border strips a couple inches longer than the quilt measurements, and then pin, sew, and trim. Done! I don't need the stress of the quilt police and as yet they have never stopped by for a visit.

Pressing seam allowances. In general, it works just fine to press seam allowances in one direction within each row, alternating the direction from row to row so that they nestle together nicely. However, I do press many of my seam allowances open to reduce bulk. You may determine the pressing direction that works best for you, depending on the weight of the fabric you're using. Sometimes the seam allowances tell me in which direction they want to lie.

Folded corners. Several patterns call for units with folded corners. When these units are used in a pattern, refer to "Making Folded Corners" below for instructions. Cut pieces the size specified in the cutting list for the project you are making.

MAKING FOLDED CORNERS

1. Lay your two fabric pieces right sides together. If the pieces are different sizes, place the smaller piece on top. Lightly draw a diagonal line from corner to corner on the wrong side of the top piece. Sew on the drawn line.

2. Trim away the corner fabric, leaving a ¼" seam allowance. You can trim both the top and bottom fabrics to reduce bulk, or trim only the top fabric, leaving the bottom fabric as a stable foundation.

3. Flip open the resulting triangle and press. If you've left the bottom fabric intact, the corners of both fabrics should align.

BAGS AND SCARF

JUST JANE

Made by Stephanie Dunphy

FINISHED BAG: 13" x 10½" x 3" deep (23" with handle)

I wanted something suitable to carry while attending my son's graduation from U.S. Army basic training, so I originally created this bag using Army camouflage print, olive-drab corduroy, and rugged, antique brass hardware. Rickrack gave a girlie touch to a utilitarian-looking bag. James noticed not only the bag but the rickrack as well. I called that bag "GI Jane." "Just Jane" is a civilian version with universal appeal.

MATERIALS

Yardage is based on 42"-wide fabric.

⅞ yard of gray dotted cotton for handles, inner pocket, lining, and button loop
½ yard of black solid corduroy for bag bottom and tabs
¼ yard of gray solid corduroy for top bands
21 squares, 5" x 5", of assorted print corduroys for patchwork
½ yard of Soft and Stable or heavyweight fusible fleece
1 yard of ½"-wide rickrack
4 O rings or similar purse hardware, 1½" diameter
4 swivel clasps, 1" x 2"
1 fantastic large button for closure

CUTTING

From *each* of the 5" squares, cut:
2 squares, 2½" x 2½" (42 total)

From the black solid corduroy, cut:
2 strips, 3¾" x 14½"
1 strip, 4½" x 13"

From the gray solid corduroy, cut:
2 strips, 3½" x 14½"

From the gray dotted cotton, cut:
2 rectangles, 12¾" x 14½"
2 strips, 3" x 30"
2 rectangles, 6½" x 8"
1 strip, 1¼" x 7"

From the Soft and Stable, cut:*
2 pieces, 15" x 16½"
*If using fusible fleece, cut 2 pieces, 12¾" x 14½".

From the rickrack, cut:
2 pieces, 16" long

The "GI Jane" bag

MAKING THE PATCHWORK UNITS

1. Arrange 21 of the assorted 2½" squares in three rows of seven squares each. With right sides together, pin and then sew the squares together into rows using a ¼" seam allowance. Press the seam allowances in opposite directions from row to row, allowing the rows to nestle together easily when joined.

2. Matching the seam intersections, pin and sew the rows together to make the front patchwork unit. Press the seam allowances in one direction. The unit should measure 6½" x 14½".

3. Repeat steps 1 and 2 with the remaining 2½" squares to make a second patchwork unit for the bag back.

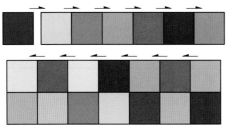

Make 2.

ASSEMBLING THE BAG BODY

1. Pin and sew a black 3¾" x 14½" strip to the bottom of each patchwork unit, right sides together. Press the seam allowances open.

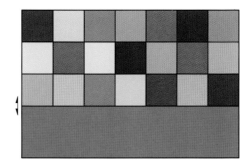

2. To make the handle tabs, press the black 4½" x 13" strip in half lengthwise, wrong sides together and raw edges aligned. Open the strip and fold both raw edges to the center crease; press. Fold the strip in half lengthwise again and press. Edgestitch along both folded edges. Trim one short end and then cut the strip into four 3"-long pieces.

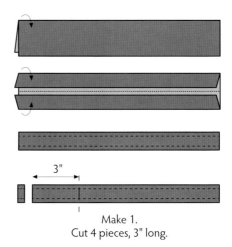

3"

Make 1.
Cut 4 pieces, 3" long.

3. Fold one tab in half with the raw edges aligned. Slip an O ring through the loop. Referring to the bag assembly diagram on page 17, place the tab along the top edge of the front patchwork unit between squares 2 and 3, aligning the raw edges. In the same way, place the second tab and ring between squares 5 and 6. Baste the tabs in place. Repeat to baste the remaining tabs on the back patchwork unit.

4. Pin and sew a gray corduroy strip along the top edge of the front patchwork unit, right sides together. Press the seam allowances toward the patchwork unit, making it easier for the tabs to point upward. Repeat for the back patchwork unit.

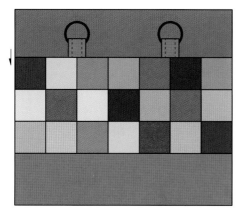

Bag assembly

5. Referring to "Soft and Stable" or "Heavyweight Fusible Fleece" on page 9, apply the stabilizer of your choice to the bag front and back. Machine quilt as desired. Trim the stabilizer even with the edges of the bag.

6. On the bag front, center and pin a piece of rickrack on the seam line between the patchwork unit and the black corduroy strip, referring to the photo on page 14 for placement guidance as needed. Sew down the center of the rickrack to secure. Trim the rickrack ends even with the edge of the bag front. Repeat to sew a piece of rickrack to the bag back.

7. With right sides together, pin the bag front and back along both sides and the bottom, matching the seam intersections. Sew around the side and bottom edges, using a ½" seam allowance. Press the seam allowances open.

8. Referring to "Making Box-Pleat Corners for Bag Bottoms" on page 10, make 1½" box-pleat corners. Leave the bag wrong side out.

ADDING THE HANDLES AND LINING

1. On the short ends of a gray dotted 30"-long strip, fold over ½" to the wrong side and press. Press the strip in half lengthwise, wrong sides together. Open the strip and fold both raw edges to the center crease; press. Fold the strip in half lengthwise again and press. Edgestitch along both folded edges to complete one handle. Repeat to make the second handle.

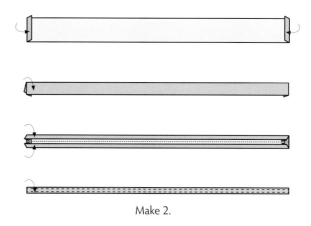

Make 2.

2. Referring to step 2 of "Assembling the Bag Body" on page 16, fold and press the gray dotted 7"-long strip to make the button loop.

3. Determine where you want to place the closure button on the bag front. Center the ends of the button loop on the bag back and adjust the length of the loop accordingly. The length of your loop will depend on your button placement. Baste in place. Trim the ends even with the edge of the bag.

4. Slip one end of a handle from step 1 through the ring of a swivel clasp, folding the end up 1" toward the back of the handle. Pin and sew, starting and stopping with a backstitch. Repeat with the other end of the handle, making sure before you start stitching that the handle isn't twisted. Complete the second handle in the same way, and then set the handles aside.

5. With right sides together and using a ¼" seam allowance, sew the gray dotted 6½" x 8" rectangles together for the pocket, leaving a 2" opening along one long side. Clip the corners, turn right side out, and press. Turn the open seam allowances under; press.

6. Pin the pocket from step 5 to the right side of a gray dotted 12¾" x 14½" rectangle, centering the pocket as shown and placing the open edge at the bottom. Edgestitch around the side and bottom edges, starting and stopping with a backstitch.

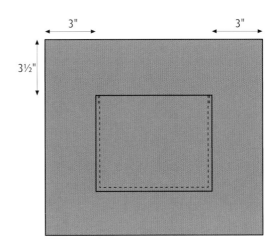

7. To make the lining, place the piece from step 6 right sides together with the remaining gray dotted 12¾" x 14½" rectangle. Using a ½" seam allowance, sew around the side and bottom edges, leaving a 5" opening along the bottom edge for turning the bag. Press the seam allowances open.

8. Make 1½" box-pleat corners and turn the lining right side out.

9. Place the lining inside of the bag, right sides together, making sure the lining pocket is facing the back loop. Matching the side seams, pin the layers together around the top edge. Sew around the top edge using a ½" seam allowance. Turn the bag right side out through the opening in the lining, and stitch the opening in the lining bottom closed. Tuck the lining neatly into the bag, leaving a peek-a-boo band of lining around the top edge. Press the top edge and stitch in the seam or ditch.

10. Attach a fantastic button and clip the handles onto the O rings.

TRAVELS WITH LOU

Made by Stephanie Dunphy

FINISHED BAG: 16½" x 13½" x 3" deep (24" with handle)

MATERIALS

Yardage is based on 42"-wide fabric.

1 yard of geometric-print cotton for handles, lining, and button loop
⅝ yard of aqua solid corduroy for bag front and back
⅝ yard of floral cotton for outer pocket, inner pocket, and bag front and back
⅛ yard of red polka-dot cotton for bag front
⅞ yard of lightweight woven fusible interfacing for handle
⅝ yard of Soft and Stable or heavyweight fusible fleece
3 coordinating medium buttons for accents
1 fantastic large button for closure

CUTTING

From the floral cotton, cut:
1 rectangle, 11½" x 18"
1 strip, 7½" x 13"
2 rectangles, 6½" x 12½"
1 strip, 3½" x 11½"

From the aqua solid corduroy, cut:
4 strips, 3" x 18"
1 strip, 2½" x 7½"
1 strip, 2½" x 11½"
1 square, 7½" x 7½"
1 rectangle, 4½" x 9½"

From the red polka-dot cotton, cut:
2 strips, 2¼" x 11½"

From the geometric-print cotton, cut:
2 rectangles, 16½" x 18"
2 strips, 7" x 25"
1 strip, 1½" x 8"

From the lightweight woven fusible interfacing, cut:
2 strips, 6½" x 24¼"

From the Soft and Stable, cut:*
2 pieces, 18" x 20"
If using fusible fleece, cut 2 pieces, 16½" x 18".

My dad has called my mother "Lou" for as long as I can remember (even though her real first name is Irma). My mother loves big purses and fills them with handy-dandy things, so I have included useful pockets both inside and out. This bag is for you, Mom!

MAKING THE BAG FRONT

1. With wrong sides together, press the floral 7½" x 13" strip in half, aligning the short ends to make the pocket. The pocket should measure 7½" x 6½".

2. Place the pocket on the right side of the aqua 7½" square, aligning the raw edges. Pin the sides, and then baste along both side edges to prevent the pocket from shifting.

3. Lay out the pocket, aqua pieces, floral strip, and red polka-dot strips as shown. Pin and then join the pieces right sides together. Press the seam allowances in the directions indicated.

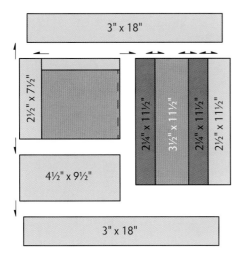

ASSEMBLING THE BAG BODY AND HANDLES

1. With right sides together, pin and sew aqua 3" x 18" strips to the top and bottom of the floral 11½" x 18" rectangle to make the bag back. Press the seam allowances toward the center.

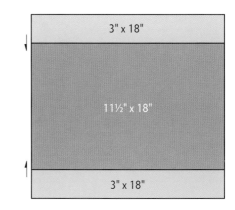

2. Referring to "Soft and Stable" or "Heavyweight Fusible Fleece" on page 9, apply the stabilizer of your choice to the bag front and back. Machine quilt as desired. Trim the stabilizer even with the edges of the bag.

3. On the bag front, decide where you want to place the accent buttons on the floral 3" strip. Sew the buttons in place. You will add the large closure button after the bag is assembled.

4. Center and fuse the interfacing to the wrong side of each geometric-print 7"-wide strip, following the manufacturer's instructions.

5. To make a handle, press one fused piece in half lengthwise, wrong sides together and raw edges aligned. Open the strip and fold both raw edges to the center crease; press. Fold the strip in half lengthwise again and press. Edgestitch along both folded edges. Repeat to make the second handle.

Accent button used for closure

6. Mark 4½" in from each side along the top edge of the bag front. With the raw edges aligned, pin the ends of one handle to the bag front. Baste in place. Baste the other handle to the bag back in the same way.

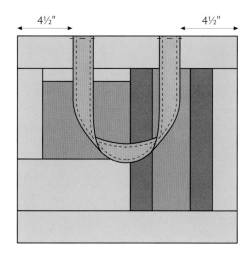

7. To make the button loop, press the geometric-print 1½" x 8" strip in half lengthwise, wrong sides together and raw edges aligned. Open the strip and fold both raw edges to the center crease; press. Fold the strip in half lengthwise again and press. Edgestitch along the open side only.

8. Determine where you want to place the closure button on the bag front. Center the ends of the button loop on the bag back and adjust the length of the loop accordingly. The length of your loop will depend on your button placement. Baste in place. Trim the ends even with the edge of the bag.

9. With right sides together, pin the bag front and back along both sides and the bottom, matching the seam intersections. Sew around the side and bottom edges, using a ½" seam allowance. Press the seam allowances open.

10. Referring to "Making Box-Pleat Corners for Bag Bottoms" on page 10, make 1½" box-pleat corners. Leave the bag wrong side out.

ADDING THE LINING

1. With right sides together and using a ¼" seam allowance, sew the floral 6½" x 12½" rectangles together for the pocket, leaving a 2" opening along one long side. Clip the corners, turn right sides out, and press. Turn the open seam allowances under; press.

2. Pin the pocket from step 1 to the right side of a geometric-print 16½" x 18" rectangle, centering the pocket as shown below and placing the open edge at the bottom. Edgestitch around the side and bottom edges, starting and stopping with a backstitch.

3. Draw a line where you would like to divide the pocket, and then sew on the line, starting and stopping with a backstitch. I divided my pocket 7" in from the left.

4. To make the lining, place the pocket piece from step 3 right sides together with the remaining geometric-print 16½" x 18" rectangle. Using a ½" seam allowance, sew around the side and bottom edges, leaving a 6" opening along the bottom edge for turning. Press the seam allowances open.

5. Make 1½" box-pleat corners and turn the lining right side out.

6. Place the lining inside of the bag, right sides together, making sure the lining pocket is facing the back loop. Matching the side seams, pin around the top edge. Sew around the top edge using a ½" seam allowance. Turn the bag right side out through the opening in the lining, and stitch the opening in the lining bottom closed. Tuck the lining neatly into the bag. Press and edgestitch around the top of the bag.

7. Attach a fantastic button.

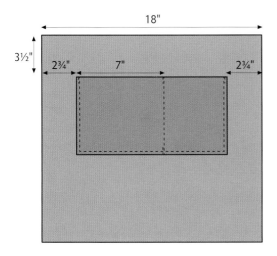

18"

3½"

2¾"   7"   2¾"

SISTER SHARON

Made by Stephanie Dunphy

FINISHED BAG: 11" x 8½" (26½" with handle)

MATERIALS

Yardage is based on 42"-wide fabric.

⅓ yard of mustard solid corduroy for bag body and handle
9" x 13" piece of teal wool for top band
⅓ yard of coordinating cotton for lining
⅓ yard of lightweight woven fusible interfacing
⅓ yard of heavyweight fusible fleece
6" length of ¹⁄₁₆"-diameter cording for button loop (such as rattail or soutache)
⅞ yard of ¾"-wide decorative ribbon
1 fantastic medium or large button for closure
4 coordinating small buttons for accents

CUTTING

From the mustard solid corduroy, cut:
2 rectangles, 6" x 12"
1 strip, 3" x 42"

From the teal wool, cut:
2 rectangles, 4" x 12"

From the cotton lining fabric, cut:
2 rectangles, 9½" x 12"

From the lightweight woven fusible interfacing, cut:
2 rectangles, 4" x 12"

From the heavyweight fusible fleece, cut:
2 rectangles, 9½" x 12"

From the decorative ribbon, cut:
2 pieces, 13" long

Sister Sharon is not a nun, but she is my sister. She always carries a small purse, one that's just big enough to hold the necessities—keys, wallet, and phone. This little purse is perfect for those days when you need just the essentials. Grab and go!

ASSEMBLING THE BAG

1. Fuse lightweight interfacing to the wrong side of each teal wool rectangle, following the manufacturer's instructions. The interfacing will help the wool keep its shape.

2. With right sides together, pin and sew a teal rectangle to the long side of a mustard rectangle, using a ¼" seam allowance. I recommend pinning very well and sewing slowly. Press the seam allowances toward the mustard rectangle. The bag front should measure 9½" x 12". Repeat to make the bag back.

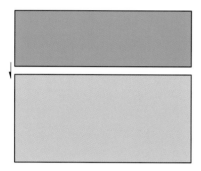

Make 2.

3. Referring to "Heavyweight Fusible Fleece" on page 9, apply fleece to the bag front and back. Machine quilt as desired.

4. Center one piece of ribbon along the seam line on the bag front. The ends of the ribbon should extend beyond the edges of the bag front. You can place the ribbon directly on the seam line, or above or below it if you wish. Pin and sew in place, stitching along the top and bottom edges of the ribbon. Stitch across both ribbon ends to prevent fraying, and then trim the ends even with the edges of the bag unit. Sew the second ribbon piece to the bag back in the same way.

5. Arrange the four small buttons on the bag front, placing them at least 2½" from the bottom edge so that they won't interfere with sewing the back and front units together. Sew the buttons in place.

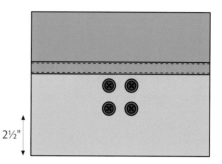

2½"

6. With right sides together, pin the bag front and back together along both sides and the bottom, matching the side seams and ribbon. Sew around the side and bottom edges, using a ½" seam allowance. Clip the corners. Press the seam allowances open, being careful not to scorch or melt the ribbon. Leave the bag wrong side out.

7. To make the handle, press the mustard corduroy 42"-long strip in half lengthwise, wrong sides together. Open the strip and fold both raw edges to the center crease; press. Fold the strip in half lengthwise again and press. Edgestitch along both folded edges.

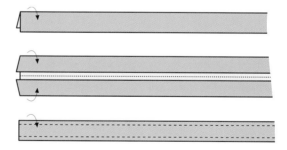

8. Center the ends of the handle on the side seams of the bag, right sides together and raw edges aligned. The handle will be on the inside of the bag. Pin and baste in place.

9. Determine where you want to place the closure button on the bag front. Fold the cording in half, center the ends of the cording on the bag back, and adjust the length of the loop accordingly. The length of your loop will depend on your button placement. Baste in place. Trim the ends even with the edge of the bag. The loop will be on the inside of the bag, facing down.

10. With right sides together, pin the lining rectangles together along both sides and the bottom. Using a ½" seam allowance, sew around the side and bottom edges, leaving a 4" opening in the bottom edge for turning. Clip the corners. Press the seam allowances open. Turn the lining right side out.

11. Place the lining inside of the bag, right sides together. Matching the side seams, pin the layers together around the top edge. Sew around the top edge using a ½" seam allowance. Turn the bag right side out through the opening in the lining, using a turning tool or chopstick to gently push out the corners. Stitch the opening in the lining bottom closed. Tuck the lining neatly into the bag. Press and edgestitch around the top of the bag.

12. Attach a fantastic button.

Funny memories of my twin aunts still make me giggle. Ethel had ruby-red lips as bright as her fuzzy red slippers. MJ preferred candy-pink lipstick that paired perfectly with her cat-eye glasses. This pattern yields twin bags— fraternal, not identical.

ETHEL AND MJ

Made by Stephanie Dunphy

FINISHED BAG: 14½" x 12" x 3" deep (20" with handle)

MATERIALS

Yardage is based on 42"-wide fabric, yields 2 bags, and allows for nap.

⅔ yard of black-and-white polka-dot corduroy for bags, handles, and button loops

⅔ yard of black-and-white houndstooth corduroy for bags, handles, and button loops

⅝ yard *each* of red dotted cotton and pink dotted cotton for linings, inner pockets, and flowers

1 yard of Soft and Stable

2 fantastic large buttons for closures

2 coordinating small or medium buttons for flower centers

CUTTING

Instructions allow for the nap to run vertically.

From *each* of the red dotted and pink dotted cottons, cut:
2 rectangles, 14" x 16½"
1 rectangle, 6½" x 13"
1 strip, 3" x 20"

From the black-and-white polka-dot corduroy, cut:
1 strip, 14" x 42"; cut into:
   2 rectangles, 7½" x 14"
   4 rectangles, 5" x 14"
   1 strip, 1½" x 7"
1 strip, 5½" x 42"

From the black-and-white houndstooth corduroy, cut:
1 strip, 14" x 42"; cut into:
   2 rectangles, 7½" x 14"
   4 rectangles, 5" x 14"
   1 strip, 1½" x 7"
1 strip, 5½" x 42"

From the Soft and Stable, cut:
4 rectangles, 16" x 18½" (2 for each bag)

MAKING THE FLOWER

The instructions that follow are for making the "Ethel" bag *only*. She is wearing red with the polka-dot center panel and the houndstooth side panels. To make the "MJ" bag, simply swap the fabric placement.

1. Place the red polka-dot strip on your ironing board with the wrong side facing up. On each short end of the strip, fold over ½" and press.

2. Press the strip in half lengthwise, wrong sides together. Thread a sewing needle and knot one end. Using a running stitch and sewing through both layers, stitch from one short end to the other end along the raw edges of the strip. When you reach the end, pull the thread to tightly gather the strip.

Raw edge

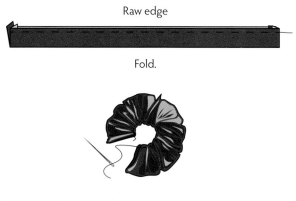

Fold.

3. Match the short folded edges of the gathered strip and whipstitch them together from end to end. Knot the thread and hide the knot by burying it between the fabric layers. Clip the thread. Set your flower aside.

ASSEMBLING THE BAG BODY

1. With right sides together and using a ¼" seam allowance, pin and sew houndstooth 5" x 14" rectangles to the long sides of a polka-dot 7½" x 14" rectangle to make the bag front. Press the seam allowances open. The bag front should measure 16½" x 14". Repeat to make the bag back.

2. Referring to "Soft and Stable" on page 9, apply the stabilizer to the bag front and back. Machine quilt as desired. Trim the stabilizer even with the edges of the bag.

3. On the bag front, place a ruler 2" in from the lower-right corner and angle it to meet the upper-right corner as shown. Cut along the ruler's edge from corner to corner. Repeat to trim the opposite side of the bag front. Cut angled corners on the bag back in the same way.

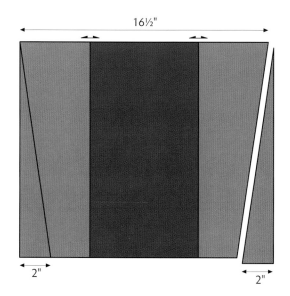

4. On the bag front, center the red flower on one seam line, 4" down from the top edge. The stitched ends should be at the back of the flower. Tack the flower to the bag using coordinating thread.

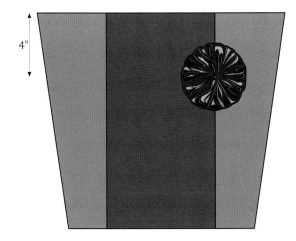

5. Sew a small or medium button in the center of the flower. The button should be large enough to cover the hole.

6. To make the handles, press the polka-dot 5½"-wide strip in half, wrong sides together and raw edges aligned. Open the strip and fold both raw edges to the center crease; press. Fold the strip in half lengthwise again and press. Edgestitch along both folded edges. Trim one short end and then cut the strip into two 19½"-long handles.

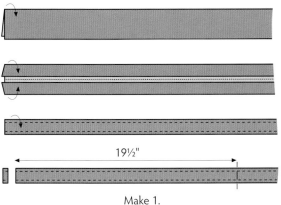
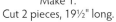

Make 1.
Cut 2 pieces, 19½" long.

7. With the raw edges aligned, center the ends of one handle on top of the seam lines on the bag front as shown. Pin and then baste in place. Baste the second handle to the bag back in the same way.

8. Repeating the procedure described in step 6, fold and press the polka-dot 1½"-wide strip to make the button loop. Edgestitch along the open side only.

9. Determine where you want to place the closure button on the bag front. Center the ends of the button loop on the bag back and adjust the length of the loop accordingly. The length of your loop will depend on your button placement. Baste in place. Trim the ends even with the edge of the bag.

10. With right sides together, pin the bag front and back along both sides and the bottom, matching the seam intersections. Sew around the side and bottom edges, using a ½" seam allowance. Press the seam allowances open.

11. Referring to "Making Box-Pleat Corners for Bag Bottoms" on page 10, make 1¼" box-pleat corners. Leave the bag wrong side out.

ADDING THE LINING

1. Fold the red dotted 6½" x 13" rectangle in half, right sides together and short ends aligned. Starting and stopping with a backstitch, use a ¼" seam allowance to sew along the raw edges, leaving a 2" opening in the center of the bottom edge for turning. Clip the corners. Turn the piece right side out and press. Press the open seam allowance under. The pocket should measure 6" x 6¼".

2. Place the red dotted 14" x 16½" rectangles right sides together. Pin along the top and bottom edges to prevent shifting. Cut the angles as described in step 3 of "Assembling the Bag Body" on page 30.

3. Pin the pocket on the right side of one lining piece, 3½" down from the top edge and centered from side to side. The open edge of the pocket should be at the bottom. Edgestitch around the side and bottom edges, starting and stopping with a backstitch.

4. Pin the lining pieces right sides together. Using a ½" seam allowance, sew around the side and bottom edges, leaving a 5" opening along the bottom edge for turning. Press the seam allowances open.

5. Make 1¼" box-pleat corners and turn the lining right side out.

6. Place the lining inside of the bag body, right sides together, making sure the lining pocket is facing the back loop. Matching the side seams, pin the layers together around the top edge. Sew around the top edge using a ½" seam allowance. Turn the bag right side out through the opening in the lining, being careful of your flower. Stitch the opening in the lining bottom closed. Tuck the lining neatly into the bag, leaving a peek-a-boo band of lining around the top edge. Press the top edge and topstitch in the seam or ditch.

7. Attach a fantastic button.

"MJ" shows an alternate colorway.

When my dog, Abby, heads to the Bed and Biscuit doggie resort, her quilt, treats, toys, and food get hauled around in a recycled plastic container, and she has been wondering when she would get her own special tote. Abby is a big girl, so she needs a big bag. Abby's two-legged friends might find this bigger tote useful for slumber parties, baby play dates, or weekend quilt retreats.

ABBY ON THE GO

Made by Stephanie Dunphy

FINISHED BAG: 20" x 18" x 3" deep (30" with handle)

MATERIALS

Yardage is based on 42"-wide fabric. For a sturdy bag, use twill, lightweight canvas, or wide-wale corduroy. Allow for extra yardage if using directional prints.

⅞ yard of paw-print cotton for bag bottom, sides, and handles
⅝ yard of dog-print cotton for bag back and inner pocket
½ yard of lime solid corduroy for bag front and back pocket
⅓ yard *total* of assorted pink polka-dot cottons for heart and ties
⅞ yard of coordinating cotton for lining
¾ yard of Soft and Stable or heavyweight fusible fleece
Alphabet and dog buttons or other novelty buttons for accents (optional)

CUTTING

From the assorted pink polka-dot cottons, cut a *total* of:
30 squares, 2½" x 2½"
2 strips, 2" x 20"

From the lime solid corduroy, cut:
1 rectangle, 7" x 14"
16 squares, 2½" x 2½"
2 rectangles, 2½" x 12½"
2 rectangles, 2½" x 16½"

From the paw-print cotton, cut:
2 strips, 4½" x 21½"
2 strips, 3" x 16½"
2 strips, 6" x 42"

From the dog-print cotton, cut:
1 strip, 16½" x 42"; cut into:
    1 rectangle, 16½" x 21½"
    1 rectangle, 16½" x 17½"

From the cotton lining fabric, cut:
1 strip, 21½" x 42"; cut into:
    1 rectangle, 20½" x 21½"
    1 rectangle, 16½" x 21½"
1 strip, 4½" x 42"; cut into 1 strip, 4½" x 21½"

From the Soft and Stable, cut:*
2 pieces, 22½" x 23½"
*If using fusible fleece, cut 2 pieces, 20½" x 21½".

MAKING THE HEART BLOCK

1. Referring to "Making Folded Corners" on page 11, use 10 pink polka-dot squares and 10 lime squares to make 10 units.

Make 10.

2. Lay out the units from step 1, the remaining pink polka-dot squares, and the remaining lime squares in six rows as shown. Sew the pieces together into rows. Press the seam allowances open.

3. Join the rows, matching seam intersections, and press. The Heart block should measure 12½" square.

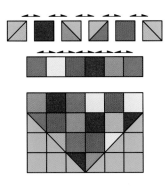

ASSEMBLING THE BAG BODY

1. With right sides together, pin and sew lime 2½" x 12½" rectangles to opposite sides of the Heart block. Pin and sew lime 2½" x 16½" rectangles to the top and bottom of the Heart block. Press all seam allowances toward the lime strips.

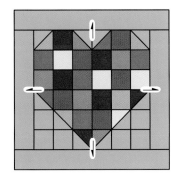

2. Pin and sew paw-print 3" x 16½" strips to opposite sides of the Heart block, right sides together. Then pin and sew a paw-print 4½" x 21½" strip to the bottom of the block to complete the bag front.

Press all seam allowances toward the just-added strips. The bag front should measure 21½" x 20½".

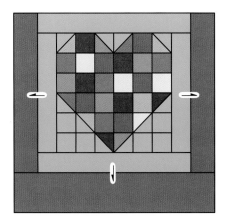

3. To make the bag back, pin and sew a paw-print 4½" x 21½" strip to the long side of the dog-print 16½" x 21½" rectangle, right sides together. Press the seam allowances toward the paw print.

4. Referring to "Soft and Stable" or "Heavyweight Fusible Fleece" on page 9, apply the stabilizer of your choice to the bag front and back. Machine quilt as desired. Trim the stabilizer even with the edges of the bag.

5. Embellish the top band on the bag front with buttons, making sure to leave 1" from the top edge so that the buttons won't get caught in the seam during bag assembly. Or, you can add the buttons after the bag is assembled.

6. To make a handle, press one paw-print 6"-wide strip in half lengthwise, wrong sides together. Open the strip and fold both raw edges to the center crease; press. Fold the strip in half lengthwise again and press. Edgestitch along both folded edges. Repeat to make the second handle. Trim the handles to 30" long.

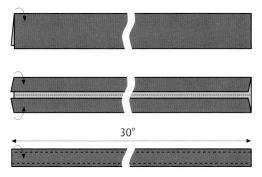

30"

Make 2.

7. Mark 6½" in from each side along the top edge of the bag front. With the raw edges aligned, pin the ends of one handle to the bag front. Baste in place. Baste the other handle to the bag back in the same way.

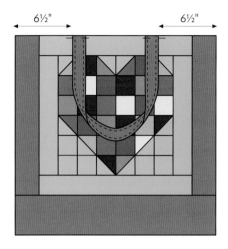

8. To make the bag ties, on one short end of a pink polka-dot strip, fold over ½" to the wrong side and press. Press the strip in half lengthwise, wrong sides together. Open the strip and fold both raw edges to the center crease; press. Fold the strip in half lengthwise again and press. Edgestitch along the folded edges. Repeat to make the second tie.

9. Mark the center along the top edge of the bag front. With the raw edges aligned, pin the end of one tie to the bag front. Baste in place. Baste the other tie to the bag back in the same way.

10. To make the outer pocket, fold the lime 7" x 14" rectangle in half, right sides together and short ends aligned. Starting and stopping with a backstitch, use a ¼" seam allowance to sew along the raw edges, leaving a 2" opening in the center of the bottom edge for turning. Clip the corners. Turn the piece right side out and press. Press the open seam allowance under. The pocket should measure 6½" x 6¾".

11. Pin the pocket on the right side of the bag back, 5½" down from the top edge and centered from side to side. The open edge of the pocket should be at the bottom. Edgestitch around the side and bottom edges, starting and stopping with a backstitch.

12. With right sides together, pin the bag front and back along both sides and the bottom, matching the seam intersections. Sew around the side and bottom edges, using a ½" seam allowance. Press the seam allowances open.

13. Referring to "Making Box-Pleat Corners for Bag Bottoms" on page 10, make 1½" box-pleat corners. Leave the bag wrong side out.

ADDING THE LINING

1. To make the lining front, sew the lining 4½" x 21½" strip to the long side of the lining 16½" x 21½" rectangle, right sides together. Press the seam allowances open. The lining front should measure 21½" x 20½".

2. Referring to step 10 of "Assembling the Bag Body" at left, use the dog-print 16½" x 17½" rectangle to make the inner pocket.

3. To make the lining back, pin the pocket on the right side of the lining 20½" x 21½" rectangle, 4" down from the 21½" edge and centered from side to side. The open edge of the pocket should be at the bottom. Edgestitch around the side and bottom edges, starting and stopping with a backstitch.

4. Lightly mark the center of the pocket from top to bottom. Sew on the line to divide the pocket, starting and stopping with a backstitch.

5. Pin the front and back lining pieces right sides together. Using a ½" seam allowance, sew around the side and bottom edges, leaving an 8" opening along the bottom edge for turning. Press the seam allowances open.

6. Make 1½" box-pleat corners and turn the lining right side out.

7. Place the lining inside of the bag, right sides together, making sure the lining pocket is facing the outer pocket. Matching the side seams, pin the layers together around the top edge. Sew around the top edge using a ½" seam allowance. Turn the bag right side out through the opening in the lining, and stitch the opening in the lining bottom closed. Tuck the lining neatly into the bag. Press and edgestitch around the top of the bag.

I think that I shall never see, a Dresden that doesn't speak to me! I heart them all. This tote has divided back pockets as well as an inner pocket. Perfect for quilt-shop hops or other getaways, it's roomy enough to hold any shopping loot or travel necessities!

I HEART DRESDENS

Made by Stephanie Dunphy

FINISHED BAG: 16" x 17½" x 3" deep (27½" with handle)

MATERIALS

Yardage is based on 42"-wide fabric.

1¼ yards of red solid corduroy for main bag and handles
1⅛ yards of red polka-dot cotton for lining, pockets, and button loop
⅓ yard of gray dotted cotton for Dresden background and inner frame
20 squares, 5" x 5", of assorted cotton prints for Dresden blades and
     squares
1 square, 5" x 5", of light-gray cotton print for circle appliqué
⅞ yard of lightweight woven fusible interfacing
⅝ yard of 1"-wide white rickrack
⅝ yard of Soft and Stable or heavyweight fusible fleece
1 fantastic button for closure
Template plastic or thin cardboard

CUTTING

Instructions allow for the nap to run vertically on the bag back.

From the gray dotted cotton, cut:
1 strip, 8½" x 42"; cut into:
     1 square, 8½" x 8½"
     2 strips, 1" x 12½"
     2 strips, 1" x 13½"

From *each* of the assorted 5" squares, cut:
2 squares, 2½" x 2½" (40 total)

From the red solid corduroy, cut:
1 rectangle, 17½" x 19½"
2 strips, 6" x 28"
1 strip, 2½" x 42"; cut into 2 strips, 2½" x 13½"
1 strip, 4" x 17½"
1 strip, 2½" x 17½"

From the red polka-dot cotton, cut:
2 strips, 17½" x 42"; cut into:
     1 rectangle, 17½" x 21"
     2 rectangles, 17½" x 19½"
     2 squares, 6" x 6"
     1 strip, 1½" x 8"

Continued on page 39

Continued from page 37

From the lightweight woven fusible interfacing, cut:
2 strips, 5½" x 27½"

From the rickrack, cut:
1 piece, 19" long

From the Soft and Stable, cut:*
2 rectangles, 19" x 21"
If using fusible fleece, cut 2 rectangles, 17½" x 19½".

MAKING THE DRESDEN BLOCK

1. Using template plastic or thin cardboard, make a template of the wedge pattern on page 42.

2. Use the template to trace a wedge on the right side of a print 2½" square. Placing a ruler on the traced lines and using a rotary cutter, cut out the wedge. Repeat to cut 20 wedges.

3. Fold a wedge shape in half lengthwise, right sides together and raw edges aligned. Begin with a backstitch at the fold and sew across the wider end, using a ¼" seam allowance. Trim the inner corner at an angle, being careful not to clip your stitches.

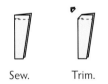

Sew. Trim.

4. Turn the wedge right side out and use a turning tool or chopstick to gently push out the tip so the piece is blade shaped. Center the seam on the back of the blade and press the seam allowances in one direction. Make 20 blades.

Make 20.

5. Starting at the fold with a backstitch, sew the blades together into pairs. Then join the pairs to make two 10-blade units. Join the units to complete the Dresden Plate. Press all seam allowances open.

6. Fold the gray 8½" square in half vertically and horizontally, and lightly crease to mark centering lines. Center the Dresden Plate on the square, aligning the seam lines with the creased lines. Pin and appliqué in place using your desired method.

7. Using heat-resistant template plastic or thin cardboard, make a template of the circle pattern on page 42. Lightly trace the circle onto the wrong side of the light-gray 5" square. Cut out the circle, adding a ¼" seam allowance. Thread a needle and knot one end. Sew a running stitch close to the outer raw edge of the circle. Place the template in the center of the fabric circle, and pull the thread to gather the seam allowance over the template. Press the edges on the front and back of the circle. Carefully remove the template and gently pull the thread to adjust the circle, if needed. Press the circle again.

8. Center the fabric circle atop the Dresden Plate. Pin or thread baste in place. Appliqué using your desired method.

MAKING THE BAG FRONT AND BACK

1. With right sides together, pin and sew four print 2½" squares together to make a short pieced strip. Press the seam allowances in one direction. Make two strips. Pin and sew six print 2½" squares together to make a long pieced strip; press. Make two of these strips.

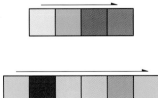

Make 2 of each.

2. With right sides together, pin and sew the short strips from step 1 to opposite sides of the Dresden Plate block. Press the seam allowances toward the center block. Pin and sew the longer pieced strips to the top and bottom of the block. Press the seam allowances toward the center block.

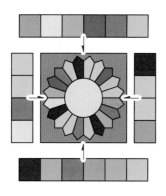

3. With right sides together, pin and sew gray 1" x 12½" strips to opposite sides of the unit from step 2. Press the seam allowances toward the gray strips. Pin and sew gray 1" x 13½" strips to the top and bottom of the unit. Press the seam allowances toward the gray strips.

4. With right sides together, pin and sew red corduroy 2½" x 13½" strips to opposite sides of the unit from step 3. Press the seam allowances toward the red strips. Pin and sew the red corduroy 2½" x 17½" strip to the top of the unit and the red corduroy 4" x 17½" strip to the bottom of the unit to complete the bag front. Press the seam allowances toward the red strips.

5. Referring to "Soft and Stable" or "Heavyweight Fusible Fleece" on page 9, apply the stabilizer of your choice to the bag front and to the red corduroy 17½" x 19" rectangle for the bag back. Machine quilt as desired. Trim the stabilizer even with the edges of the bag.

6. To make the outside pocket, fold the red polka-dot 17½" x 21" rectangle in half lengthwise, right sides together and raw edges aligned. Sew along the long raw edge using a ¼" seam allowance. Press the seam allowances open and turn the pocket right side out. Lay the pocket flat on your ironing board with the seam centered on the back; press the top and bottom folds. The seam allowance will be on the inside of the pocket.

7. On the right side of the pocket, lay the white rickrack piece along the top folded edge of the pocket with the rickrack bumps even with the fold. The rickrack ends should extend beyond the edges of the pocket. Pin the rickrack in place and then stitch through the center.

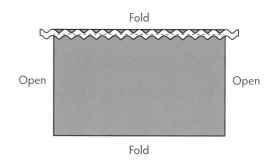

8. Place the pocket on the bag back 4½" from the top edge, with the side raw edges aligned. Pin and then baste along the sides edges. Trim the rickrack even with the edge of the bag. Edgestitch along the bottom of the pocket.

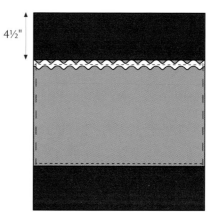

9. Lightly draw a line 9½" in from the left edge to divide the pocket in half. Sew on the drawn line, beginning at the bottom and starting and stopping with a backstitch.

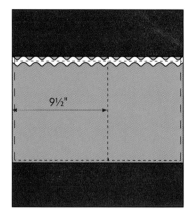

ASSEMBLING THE BAG

1. Center and apply fusible interfacing to the wrong side of each red corduroy 6"-wide strip, following the manufacturer's instructions.

2. To make a handle, press a red strip from step 1 in half lengthwise, wrong sides together. Open the strip and fold both raw edges to the center crease; press. Fold the strip in half lengthwise again and press. Edgestitch along both folded edges. Repeat to make the second handle.

3. Mark 4½" in from each side along the top edge of the bag front. With the raw edges aligned, pin the ends of one handle to the bag front. Baste in place. Baste the other handle to the bag back in the same way.

4. To make the button loop, press the red polka-dot 1½" x 8" strip in half lengthwise, wrong sides together. Open the strip and fold both raw edges to the center crease; press. Fold the strip in half lengthwise again and press. Edgestitch along the open side only.

5. Determine where you want to place the closure button on the bag front. Center the ends of the button loop on the bag back and adjust the length of the loop accordingly. The length of your loop will depend on your button placement. Baste in place. Trim the ends even with the edge of the bag.

6. With right sides together, pin the bag front and back along both sides and the bottom. Sew around the side and bottom edges, using a ½" seam allowance. Press the seam allowances open.

7. Referring to "Making Box-Pleat Corners for Bag Bottoms" on page 10, make 1½" box-pleat corners. Leave the bag wrong side out.

ADDING THE LINING

1. With right sides together and using a ¼" seam allowance, sew the red polka-dot 6" squares together for the pocket, leaving a 2" opening along one side. Clip the corners, turn right side out, and press. Turn the open seam allowances under; press.

2. Pin the pocket from step 1 to the right side of a red polka-dot 17½" x 19½" rectangle, 4" down from the 17½" edge and centered from side to side. The open edge of the pocket should be at the bottom. Edgestitch around the side and bottom edges, starting and stopping with a backstitch.

3. To make the lining, place the piece from step 2 right sides together with the remaining red polka-dot 17½" x 19½" rectangle. Using a ½" seam allowance, sew around the side and bottom edges, leaving a 6" opening along the bottom edge for turning the bag. Press the seam allowances open.

4. Make 1½" box-pleat corners and turn the lining right side out.

5. Place the lining inside of the bag, right sides together, making sure the lining pocket is facing the back loop. Matching the side seams, pin the layers together around the top edge. Sew around the top edge using a ½" seam allowance. Turn the bag right side out through the opening in the lining, and stitch the opening in the lining bottom closed. Tuck the lining neatly into the bag. Press and edgestitch around the top of the bag.

6. Attach a fantastic button.

Appliqué pattern does not include seam allowance. Add ¼" for turned-edge appliqué.

Circle
Make 1.

Wedge
Make 20.

¼" seam allowance

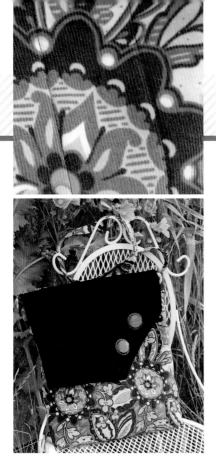

California Girl Bag and Scarf are the perfect pair for a casual outing.

Made by Stephanie Dunphy

California Girl Bag

FINISHED BAG: 14½" x 14" x 2" deep (32" with handle)

Picture this: a small-town California girl in the early 1970s, navy-blue corduroy bell-bottom pants, and a blue-green-and-white crocheted granny-square vest over a mint-green blouse. The perfect addition was my navy-blue suede clogs. I wish I'd had this bag to finish off the outfit! "California Girl" has an inner pocket as well as a pocket just under the flap. Sling it over your shoulder and take the road less traveled.

MATERIALS

Yardage is based on 42"-wide fabric.

⅞ yard of blue print corduroy for bag body, handle, and lining pocket
⅝ yard of dark-blue solid corduroy for bag flap and pocket
½ yard of coordinating cotton for lining
⅝ yard of heavyweight fusible fleece
2 fantastic large buttons for accents

CUTTING

From the dark-blue solid corduroy, cut:
1 strip, 11½" x 42"; cut into 2 rectangles, 11½" x 13½"
1 rectangle, 5½" x 11½"

From the blue print corduroy, cut:
1 strip, 16" x 42"; cut into 2 rectangles, 15½" x 16"
1 rectangle, 7½" x 13"
1 strip, 3" x 42"

From the cotton lining fabric, cut:
2 rectangles, 15½" x 16"

From the heavyweight fusible fleece, cut:
2 rectangles, 15½" x 16"
1 rectangle, 11½" x 13½"

ASSEMBLING THE BAG BODY

1. Apply the fusible fleece 11½" x 13½" rectangle to the wrong side of one dark-blue 11½" x 13½" rectangle, following the manufacturer's instructions.

2. Position the fused rectangle right side up with the 13½" edges at the top and bottom. Place the second dark-blue 11½" x 13½" rectangle on top of the fused piece, right sides together. Pin along all sides to prevent shifting. Along the bottom edge, mark 8" in from the lower-left corner and 5½" down from the upper-right corner as shown. Align the edge of a ruler with the marks, and cut along the ruler's edge through all the layers.

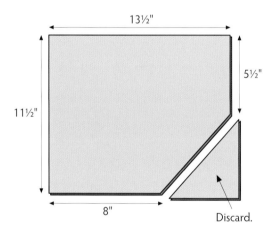

3. Using a ½" seam allowance, sew around the sides, angled edge, and bottom, leaving the top 13½" edge open to make the flap. Clip the corners. Turn the flap right side out, using a turning tool or chopsticks to gently push out the corners. Align the top raw edges and press. Pin the open edges together to keep them from shifting, and machine quilt as desired. After machine quilting, baste along the raw edges, making sure they are still aligned.

4. Referring to "Heavyweight Fusible Fleece" on page 9, apply a fleece 15½" x 16" rectangle to the wrong side of each blue-print 15½" x 16" rectangle. Machine quilt as desired. One quilted rectangle is the bag front, the other is the bag back.

5. To make a pocket, fold the dark-blue 5½" x 11½" rectangle in half, right sides together and short ends aligned. Starting and stopping with a backstitch, use a ¼" seam allowance to sew along the raw edges, leaving a 2" opening in the center of the bottom edge for turning. Clip the corners. Turn the piece right side out and press. Press the open seam allowance under. The pocket should measure 5" x 5¾". In the same way, use the blue-print 7½" x 13" rectangle to make a 7" x 6½" lining pocket.

6. Pin the dark-blue pocket on the right side of the bag front, 2½" down from the top edge and 3" in from the left edge. The open edge of the pocket should be at the bottom. Edgestitch around the side and bottom edges, starting and stopping with a backstitch.

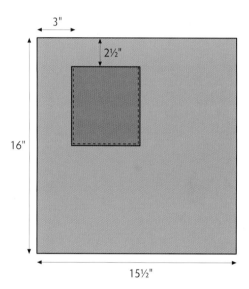

7. With right sides together, pin the bag front and back along both sides and the bottom. Sew around the side and bottom edges, using a ½" seam allowance. Press the seam allowances open.

8. Referring to "Making Box-Pleat Corners for Bag Bottoms" on page 10, make 1" box-pleat corners. Leave the bag wrong side out.

9. Center the bag flap on the bag back, right sides together and raw edges aligned. Pin and then baste in place. The flap will be inside the bag.

11. Center the ends of the handle on the side seams of the bag, right sides together and raw edges aligned. The handle will be on the inside of the bag. Pin and baste in place.

ADDING THE LINING

1. Pin the lining pocket on the right side of one lining 15½" x 16" rectangle, 4" down from the top edge and centered from side to side as shown. The open edge of the pocket should be at the bottom. Edgestitch around the side and bottom edges, starting and stopping with a backstitch.

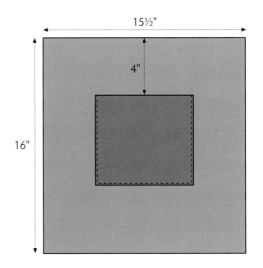

2. To make the lining, place the piece from step 1 right sides together with the remaining lining rectangle. Using a ½" seam allowance, sew around the side and bottom edges, leaving a 6" opening along the bottom edge for turning. Press the seam allowances open.

3. Make 1" box-pleat corners and turn the lining right side out.

4. Place the lining inside of the bag, right sides together, making sure the lining pocket is facing the flap. Matching the side seams, pin the layers together around the top edge. Sew around the top edge using a ½" seam allowance. Turn the bag right side out through the opening in the lining, and stitch the opening in the lining bottom closed. Tuck the lining neatly into the bag. Press and edgestitch around the top of the bag.

5. Attach two fantastic buttons along the angle of the flap.

10. To make the handle, press the blue-print 3"-wide strip in half lengthwise, wrong sides together. Open the strip and fold both raw edges to the center crease; press. Fold the strip in half lengthwise again and press. Edgestitch along both folded edges.

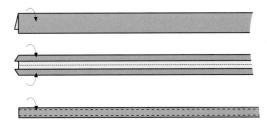

California Girl Scarf

FINISHED SCARF: 6" x 70"

Warm, soft, pretty, and so simple, this cozy scarf can be yours in an hour! The yardage requirements allow you to make two scarves, one for you and one for a friend.

MATERIALS

Yardage is based on 42"-wide fabric, yields 2 scarves, and allows for nap.

1⅞ yards of blue print corduroy for main scarf
½ yard of dark-blue solid corduroy for scarf ends
12 small, pretty buttons for accents

CUTTING

Instructions allow for the nap to go in one direction.

From the blue print corduroy, cut on the *lengthwise grain*:
2 strips, 13" x 59"

From the dark-blue solid corduroy, cut:
2 strips, 7" x 42"; cut into 4 rectangles, 7" x 13"

ASSEMBLING THE SCARF

Instructions are for making one scarf.

1. With right sides together, pin and sew dark-blue rectangles to both short ends of the blue-print strip as shown, using a ½" seam allowance. Press the seam allowances open.

2. Fold the scarf in half lengthwise, right sides together, matching the seam intersections and raw edges. Pin both short ends and along the long side. Using a ½" seam allowance and starting and stopping with a backstitch, sew around the raw edges, leaving an 8" opening in the middle of the long side for turning.

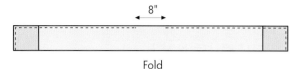

8"

Fold

3. Clip the corners and turn the scarf right side out through the opening. Use a turning tool or chopstick to gently push out the corners. Turn the open seam allowances under; press. Press around all sides. Pin the opening closed.

4. Edgestitch around the scarf, starting and stopping with a backstitch.

5. Sew three small, pretty buttons to each scarf end.

QUILTS

SCOOTER BUG

Pieced by Stephanie Dunphy and quilted by Jackie Kunkel

FINISHED QUILT: 35½" x 41½" ◆ FINISHED BLOCK: 6" x 6"

MATERIALS

Yardage is based on 42"-wide fabric. Fat quarters measure 18" x 21".

10 fat quarters of assorted print flannels for blocks and pieced backing
1 yard of berry solid corduroy for blocks, binding, and tag-along tab
1 yard of print flannel for outer border and pieced backing
⅓ yard of cream solid corduroy for inner border
41" x 47" piece of batting

CUTTING

From *each* of 8 flannel fat quarters, cut:
2 strips, 2½" x 21" (16 total)
1 rectangle, 10⅞" x 21" (8 total)

From *each* of 2 flannel fat quarters, cut:
2 strips, 2½" x 21" (4 total)

From the berry solid corduroy, cut:
10 strips, 1½" x 42"; cut into 20 strips, 1½" x 21"
5 strips, 3" x 42"
1 strip, 2" x 9" (optional; for tag-along tag)

From the cream solid corduroy, cut:
4 strips, 2" x 42"

From the print flannel, cut:
4 strips, 4½" x 42"
1 strip, 11½" x 42"

"Scooter Bug"—a toddler tag-along quilt—is a combination of my children's childhood nicknames. Little ones can enjoy sweet dreams under a cozy combination of corduroy and flannel. Nap time never felt so good!

MAKING THE BLOCKS

1. With right sides together, pin and sew one berry 21"-long strip to the long edge of one flannel 21"-long strip to make a strip set. Press the seam allowances toward the berry strip. Make a total of 20 strip sets. From each strip set, cut four 3½"-wide segments (80 total).

3½"

Make 20 strip sets.
Cut 4 segments, 3½" wide, from each strip set (80 total).

2. Lay out four matching segments from step 1, rotating them as shown. With right sides together, pin and sew the segments together in rows. Press the seam allowances open. Join the rows, matching the seam intersection, to complete the block. Press the seam allowances open. Repeat to make a total of 20 blocks.

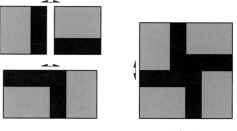

Make 20.

Mix It Up
You can mix up the segments in each block if you want a less controlled look. Have fun!

ASSEMBLING THE QUILT TOP

1. Arrange the blocks in five rows of four blocks each. Pin and sew the blocks into rows, matching the seam intersections. Press the seam allowances open.

2. Pin and sew the rows together, matching the seam intersections, to complete the quilt center. Press the seam allowances open.

3. To add the inner border, pin and sew cream corduroy strips to opposite sides of the quilt center. Press the seam allowances toward the strips. Trim the ends even with the quilt edges. Pin and sew cream corduroy strips to the top and bottom of the quilt center to complete the inner border. Press the seam allowances toward the border strips and trim the ends even with the quilt edges.

4. To add the outer border, pin and sew flannel 4½"-wide strips to opposite sides of the quilt. Press the seam allowances toward the flannel strips. Trim the ends even with the quilt edges. Pin and sew flannel 4½"-wide strips to the top and bottom of the quilt to complete the outer border. Press the

seam allowances toward the flannel strips and trim the ends even with the quilt edges.

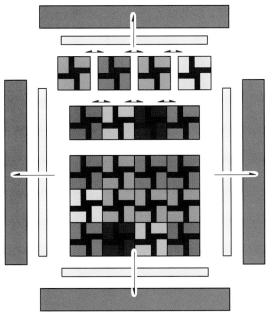

Quilt assembly

FINISHING THE QUILT

Visit ShopMartingale.com/HowtoQuilt to download free illustrated information on finishing techniques.

1. To make the quilt back, join four flannel 10⅞" x 21" rectangles side by side to make a 21" x 42" strip. Press the seam allowances open. Repeat to make a second pieced strip. Pin and sew the pieced strips and the flannel 11½" x 42" strip together as shown. Press the seam allowances open.

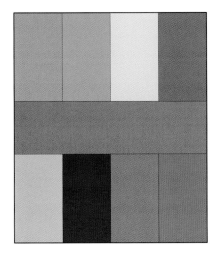

Alternate "Scooter Bug" colorways

An optional tag-a-long tab for sweet little hands.

2. Layer the backing, batting, and quilt top; baste.

3. Quilt as desired.

4. Trim the backing and batting even with the quilt top.

5. To make the optional tag-along tab, press the berry 2" x 9" strip in half lengthwise, wrong sides together. Open the strip and fold both raw edges to the center crease; press. Fold the strip in half lengthwise again and press. Edgestitch along the open edge.

6. On the back of the quilt, place the tag-along tab diagonally in one upper corner, 5" down and 5" across from the corner as shown. The tab will extend beyond the edges of the quilt. Pin and sew in place, stitching about ⅛" from the outer edges. Trim the tab even with the quilt edges.

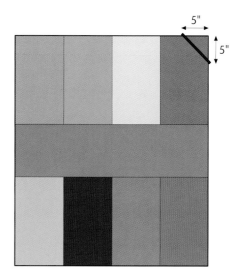

7. Using the berry 3"-wide strips, make and attach binding. When sewing the binding to the back of quilt, take extra care to secure the binding where it overlaps the tab, as this will be a stress point. I recommend sewing extra stitches; you can also machine stitch across the tab from either the front or back of the quilt.

8. Don't forget your label!

FAIRLANE

Pieced by Stephanie Dunphy and quilted by Jane Williams

FINISHED QUILT: 50½" x 60½" ◆ FINISHED BLOCK: 10" x 10"

MATERIALS

Yardage is based on 42"-wide fabric.

3 yards of black solid corduroy for blocks
1¼ yards of multicolored striped cotton for blocks and binding
⅓ yard *each* of red solid and aqua solid corduroy for blocks
3¼ yards of fabric for backing
56" x 66" piece of batting

CUTTING

From the black solid corduroy, cut:
20 strips, 4¾" x 42"; cut into 60 rectangles, 4¾" x 10½"

From the multicolored striped cotton, cut:
10 strips, 2" x 42"; cut into 30 rectangles, 2" x 10½"
6 strips, 3" x 42"

From the red solid corduroy, cut:
3 strips, 2½" x 42"; cut into 40 squares, 2½" x 2½"

From the aqua solid corduroy, cut:
3 strips, 2½" x 42"; cut into 40 squares, 2½" x 2½"

MAKING THE BLOCKS

1. With right sides together, pin and sew black corduroy rectangles to the long edges of a striped rectangle. Press the seam allowances toward the center. The block should measure 10½" square. Repeat to make a total of 30 blocks.

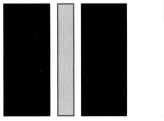

Make 30.

Dad drove a 1966 Ford Fairlane 500 for more than 40 years before finally selling his beloved car. That was the car of my childhood. Dad's cars are always white with black interior—classy, just like Dad.

2. Referring to "Making Folded Corners" on page 11, sew a red square to a block from step 1 as shown to make block A. Make two of block A.

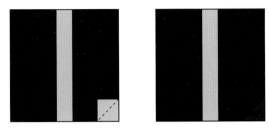

Block A.
Make 2.

3. In the same way, sew red and aqua squares to the remaining blocks to make two of block B, seven of block C, seven of block D, and 12 of block E, making sure to note the direction of the striped rectangle in each block.

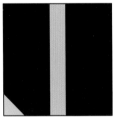

Block B.
Make 2.

Block C.
Make 7.

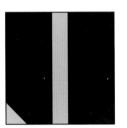
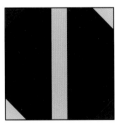

Block D.
Make 7.

Block E.
Make 12.

ASSEMBLING THE QUILT TOP

1. Lay out the blocks in six rows of five blocks each, alternating and rotating the blocks as shown in the quilt assembly diagram below. Pin and sew the blocks together into rows. Press the seam allowances open.

2. Join the rows, matching the seam intersections. Press the seam allowances open.

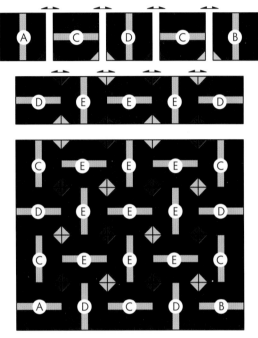

Quilt assembly

FINISHING THE QUILT

Visit ShopMartingale.com/HowtoQuilt to download free illustrated information on finishing techniques.

1. Layer the backing, batting, and quilt top; baste.

2. Quilt as desired.

3. Trim the backing and batting even with the quilt top.

4. Using the striped 3"-wide strips, make and attach binding.

5. Don't forget your label!

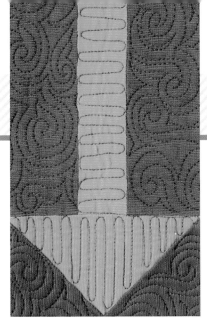

My sister, Sharon, is Grammy to three adorable grandchildren. They often call her and ask to spend the night. The arrows represent the fact that *all* roads lead to Grammy's house. Where will your arrows lead?

GOIN' TO GRAMMY'S

Pieced by Stephanie Dunphy and quilted by Jane Williams

FINISHED QUILT: 44½" x 56½" ◆ FINISHED BLOCK: 12" x 16"

MATERIALS

Yardage is based on 42"-wide fabric.

1¾ yards of owl-print corduroy for border and pieced backing
1⅔ yards of camel solid corduroy for block backgrounds
⅞ yard of white polka-dot corduroy for blocks and binding
⅜ yard *each* of orange solid, blue solid, and green solid corduroy
    for blocks
1¾ yards of coordinating corduroy for pieced backing
50" x 63" piece of batting

Make It Scrappy

If you want to make a scrappy version, one 2½" x 42" strip and one 1½" x 42" strip will yield six arrow units.

CUTTING

From the camel solid corduroy, cut:
7 strips, 2½" x 42"; cut into 108 squares, 2½" x 2½"
18 strips, 2" x 42"; cut into 108 rectangles, 2" x 6½"

From the white polka-dot corduroy, cut:
2 strips, 1½" x 42"; cut into 9 rectangles, 1½" x 6½"
2 strips, 2½" x 42"; cut into 9 rectangles, 2½" x 4½"
6 strips, 3" x 42"

From *each* of the orange solid, blue solid, and green solid corduroys, cut:
3 strips, 1½" x 42"; cut into 15 rectangles, 1½" x 6½" (45 total)
2 strips, 2½" x 42"; cut into 15 rectangles, 2½" x 4½" (45 total)

From the *lengthwise grain* of the owl-print corduroy, cut:
4 strips, 4½" x 63"
1 piece, 21" x 63"

From the *lengthwise grain* of the coordinating corduroy for backing, cut:
2 pieces, 16" x 63"

MAKING THE BLOCKS

1. Referring to "Making Folded Corners" on page 11, sew camel squares to a white 2½" x 4½" rectangle to make an arrow-point unit. Make nine units.

Make 9.

2. With right sides together, pin and sew camel 2" x 6½" rectangles to the long edges of a white 1½" x 6½" rectangle. Press the seam allowances open. Sew an arrow-point unit to the top of the strip-pieced unit to complete an arrow unit. Press the seam allowances open. The unit should measure 4½" x 8½". Make a total of nine white arrow units.

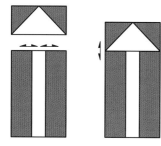

Make 9.

3. Repeat steps 1 and 2 to make 15 blue, 15 orange, and 15 green arrow units.

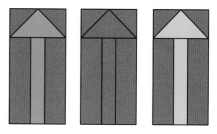

Make 15 of each.

4. Pin and sew six arrow units together as shown to make a block. Press the seam allowances open. The block should measure 12½" x 16½". Make a total of nine blocks, referring to the quilt assembly diagram on page 61 and the photo at left for color placement guidance.

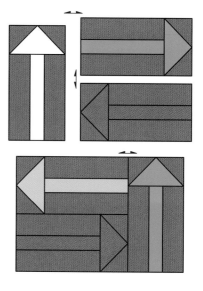

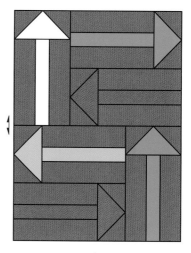

Make 9.

ASSEMBLING THE QUILT TOP

1. Arrange the blocks in three rows of three blocks each. Pin and sew the blocks together into rows, matching the seam intersections. Press the seam allowances open.

2. Sew the rows together, matching the seam intersections. Press the seam allowances open.

3. To add the border, pin and sew owl-print 4½"-wide strips to opposite sides of the quilt center. Press the seam allowances toward the strips. Trim the ends even with the quilt edges. Pin and sew owl-print 4½"-wide strips to the top and bottom of the quilt center to complete the border. Press the seam allowances toward the border strips and trim the ends even with the quilt edges.

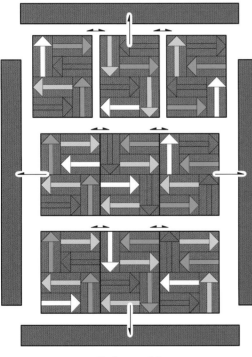

Quilt assembly

FINISHING THE QUILT

Visit ShopMartingale.com/HowtoQuilt to download free illustrated information on finishing techniques.

1. To make the backing, sew the corduroy 16" x 63" pieces to opposite sides of the owl-print 21" x 63" piece, using a ½" seam allowance. Press the seam allowances open.

2. Layer the backing, batting, and quilt top; baste.

3. Quilt as desired.

4. Trim the backing and batting even with the quilt top.

5. Using the white 3"-wide strips, make and attach binding.

6. Don't forget your label!

Dresden Plate blocks are my signature. I see them everywhere. My inspiration for these quilts came from the roof of our neighborhood gazebo. "Mr. and Mrs. D." represent the mister and me.

MR. AND MRS. D.

Pieced by Stephanie Dunphy and quilted by Linda Hrcka

Mr. D.

FINISHED QUILT: 64½" x 64½"

MATERIALS

Yardage is based on 42"-wide fabric.

3¼ yards of light-gray print cotton for background and large Dresden Plate
2 yards of medium-gray solid corduroy for background
⅞ yard of dark-gray solid corduroy for small Dresden Plate and binding
6" x 6" square of pale-gray print cotton for circle appliqué
4⅛ yards of fabric for backing
70" x 70" piece of batting
Template plastic or thin cardboard

CUTTING

From the *crosswise grain* of the light-gray print cotton, cut:
2 strips, 12" x 42"

From the *lengthwise grain* of the light-gray print cotton, cut:
8 strips, 4½" x 83"; cut into:
    2 strips, 4½" x 64½"
    4 strips, 4½" x 28½"
    4 strips, 4½" x 24½"
    4 strips, 4½" x 20½"
    4 strips, 4½" x 16½"
    4 strips, 4½" x 12½"
    4 strips, 4½" x 8½"
    4 squares, 4½" x 4½"

From the *lengthwise grain* of the medium-gray solid corduroy, cut:
8 strips, 4½" x 66"; cut into:
    2 strips, 4½" x 56½"
    2 strips, 4½" x 48½"
    2 strips, 4½" x 40½"
    2 strips, 4½" x 32½"
    2 strips, 4½" x 24½"
    2 strips, 4½" x 16½"
    2 strips, 4½" x 8½"

Continued on page 64

Continued from page 63

From the dark-gray solid corduroy, cut:
1 strip, 6" x 42"
7 strips, 3" x 42"

ASSEMBLING THE QUILT CENTER

1. Using a design wall or other flat surface, lay out the light-gray 4½"-wide strips and medium-gray corduroy strips as shown below. With right sides together, pin and sew the strips together into rows. Press the seam allowances open. Each row should measure 4½" x 64½".

2. Pin and sew the rows together, adding light-gray 4½"-wide strips to the top and bottom of the quilt center. Press the seam allowances open. You may find it easier to assemble the quilt center in four sections and then join the sections. The quilt center should measure 64½" square.

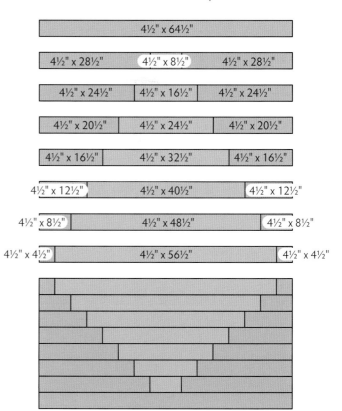

Quilt assembly

*The gazebo roof that inspired
this pair of quilt designs*

MAKING THE DRESDEN PLATES

1. Using template plastic or thin cardboard, make templates of the wedge patterns on pages 68 and 69.

2. Use template A to trace six wedges on the right side of each light-gray 12"-wide strip, rotating the template as shown. Placing a ruler on the traced lines and using a rotary cutter, cut out a total of 12 wedges.

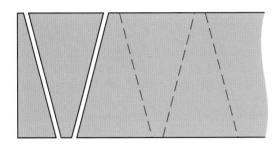

3. Fold each wedge shape in half lengthwise, right sides together and raw edges aligned. Begin with a backstitch at the fold and sew across the wider end, using a ¼" seam allowance. Trim the inner corner at an angle, being careful not to clip your stitches.

Sew.   Trim.

4. Turn the wedge right side out and use a turning tool or chopstick to gently push out the tip so the piece is blade shaped. Center the seam on the back of the blade and press the seam allowance in one direction. Make 12 blades.

Make 12.

5. Starting at the fold with a backstitch, sew the blades together into pairs. Then join the pairs to make two six-blade units. Join the units to complete the large Dresden Plate. Press all seam allowances open.

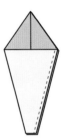

6. Use template B to trace 12 wedges on the right side of the dark-gray 6"-wide strip. Cut out the wedges. Repeat steps 3–5 to make a small Dresden Plate.

APPLIQUÉING THE DRESDEN PLATES

Refer to the appliqué placement diagram on page 66 as needed.

1. Lay the pressed quilt center on a flat surface. Measure 32¼" from each outer edge and mark centering lines on the medium-gray background.

2. Center the large Dresden Plate on the quilt center with the blade tips on the centering lines. Pin and then baste in place.

3. Center the small Dresden Plate on top of the large Dresden Plate with the tip of a blade on each seam line. Pin and then baste in place.

4. Appliqué both Dresden Plates in place using your desired method.

Appliqué placement

5. Using heat-resistant template plastic or thin cardboard, make a template of the circle pattern on page 69. Lightly trace the circle onto the wrong side of the pale-gray 6" square. Cut out the circle, adding a ¼" seam allowance. Thread a needle and knot one end. Sew a running stitch close to the outer raw edge of the circle. Place the template in the center of the fabric circle, and pull the thread to gather the seam allowance over the template. Press the edges on the front and back of the circle. Carefully remove the template and gently pull the thread to adjust the circle, if needed. Press the circle again.

6. Center the fabric circle atop the small Dresden Plate. Pin or baste in place. Appliqué using your desired method.

FINISHING THE QUILT

Visit ShopMartingale.com/HowtoQuilt to download free illustrated information on finishing techniques.

1. Layer the backing, batting, and quilt top; baste.

2. Quilt as desired.

3. Trim the backing and batting even with the quilt top.

4. Using the dark-gray 3"-wide strips, make and attach binding.

5. Don't forget your label!

Mrs. D.

FINISHED QUILT: 64½" X 64½"

MATERIALS

Yardage is based on 42"-wide fabric.

3¼ yards of black dotted cotton for background

2 yards of teal solid corduroy for background

½ yard *total* of 5 or 6 assorted yellow print cottons for large Dresden Plate

½ yard *total* of 3 assorted black print cottons for large Dresden Plate and appliquéd circle

¼ yard of aqua print cotton for small Dresden Plate

⅔ yard of coordinating cotton for binding

4⅛ yards of fabric for backing

70" x 70" piece of batting

CUTTING

Follow the cutting instructions on pages 63 and 64 of "Mr. D.," with the following changes:

- Substitute assorted yellow prints and assorted black prints for the light-gray 12"-wide strips cut on the crosswise grain.
- Substitute black dotted cotton for the light-gray 4½"-wide strips cut on the lengthwise grain.
- Substitute teal solid corduroy for the medium-gray 4½"-wide strips.
- Substitute aqua print cotton for the dark-gray 6"-wide strip.
- Substitute coordinating cotton for the dark-gray 3"-wide strips.

ASSEMBLING THE QUILT

Assemble the quilt as described on pages 64–66.

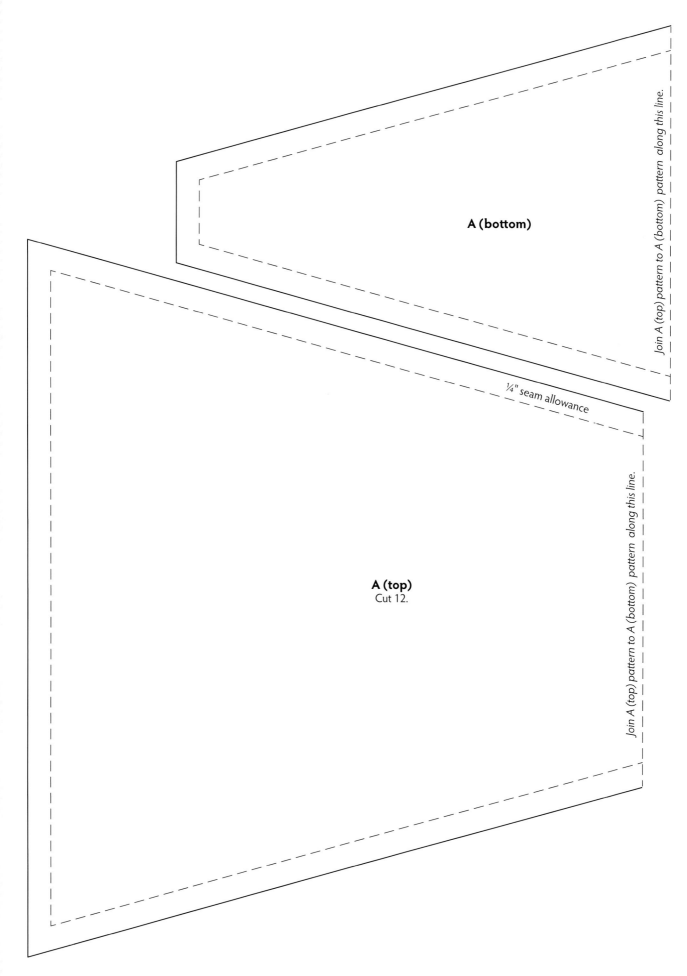

A (bottom)

Join A (top) pattern to A (bottom) pattern along this line.

¼" seam allowance

A (top)
Cut 12.

Join A (top) pattern to A (bottom) pattern along this line.

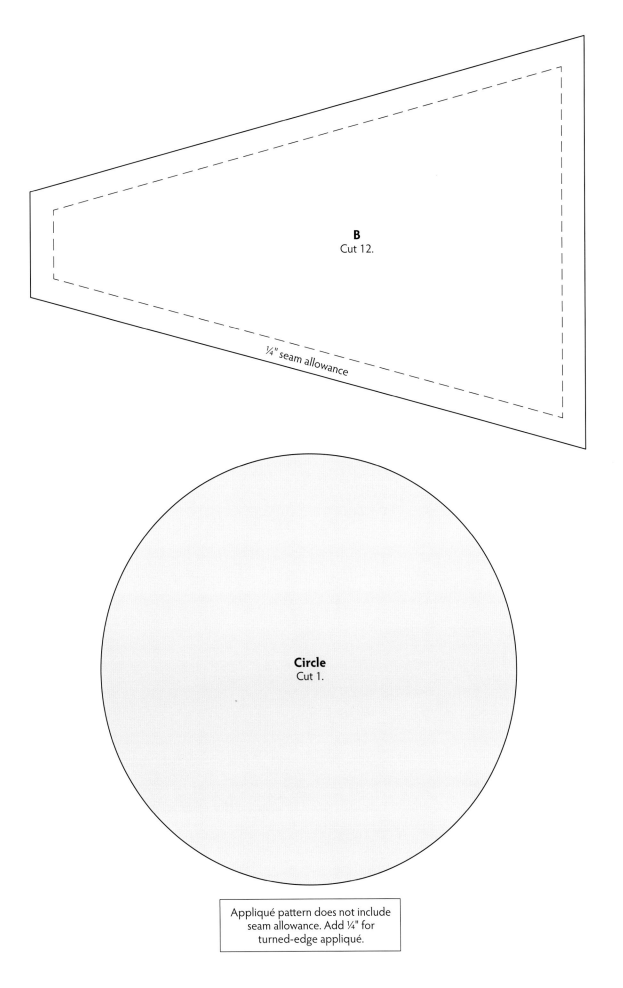

B
Cut 12.

¼" seam allowance

Circle
Cut 1.

Appliqué pattern does not include
seam allowance. Add ¼" for
turned-edge appliqué.

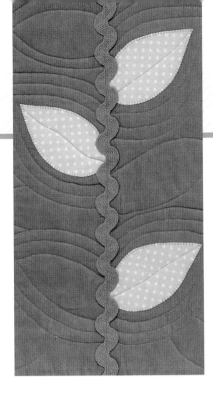

LITTLE SPROUT

Pieced and quilted by Stephanie Dunphy

FINISHED QUILT: 32½" x 37½"

My journey into pattern design started when I designed my first bag in 2009. This quilt pays tribute to the way I've nurtured my business as a little sprout and watched it grow.

MATERIALS

Yardage is based on 42"-wide fabric.

½ yard of turquoise corduroy for leaf panel
½ yard of chocolate dotted corduroy for borders
¼ yard *each* of 5 assorted print cottons for strip-pieced panel
6" x 10" scrap of green print cotton for leaves
½ yard of multicolored striped cotton for binding
1⅓ yards of fabric for backing
38" x 43" piece of batting
¾ yard of lightweight woven fusible interfacing
⅞ yard of 1"-wide tan rickrack
6" x 10" square of fusible web
Template plastic or thin cardboard
Chalk pencil or other fabric-marking tool

CUTTING

From the turquoise corduroy, cut:
1 strip, 12½" x 25½"

From *each* of the assorted print cottons, cut:
1 strip, 5½" x 20½" (5 total)

From the chocolate dotted corduroy, cut:
2 strips, 6½" x 32½"

From the multicolored striped cotton, cut:
4 strips, 3" x 42"

From the lightweight woven fusible interfacing, cut:
1 strip, 8" x 22"

APPLIQUÉING THE LEAVES

1. Center and apply the 8" x 22" strip of fusible interfacing on the wrong side of the turquoise strip, following the manufacturer's instructions.

2. Using a chalk pencil or other marking tool, lightly mark the lengthwise center of the turquoise strip. Place the piece of rickrack on top of the center line, with the ends extending beyond the edges of the turquoise strip as shown below. Pin in place.

3. Using template plastic or thin cardboard, make a template of the leaf pattern on page 73. Use the template to trace four leaves onto the paper side of the fusible web. Cut out the fusible-web leaves, leaving about ¼" all around the marked lines. Fuse the leaves to the wrong side of the green cotton rectangle, following the manufacturer's instructions.

4. Cut out the leaves on the drawn line and remove the paper backing. Position the leaves along the rickrack, tucking them under the rickrack bumps as shown. When you are pleased with the arrangement, fuse the leaves in place. If your rickrack is not 100% cotton, move the rickrack out of the way before pressing so that you don't scorch or melt it.

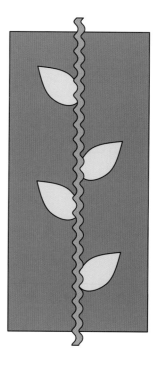

5. Machine stitch through the center of the rickrack. Machine or hand blanket-stitch around the outer edges of the leaves. Trim the rickrack tails even with the edges of the turquoise strip.

ASSEMBLING THE QUILT TOP

1. Pin and sew the assorted 5½" x 20½" strips together along their long edges. Press the seam allowances open. The pieced section should measure 20½" x 25½".

2. Referring to the quilt assembly diagram, pin and sew the appliquéd strip to the pieced section from step 1. Press the seam allowances toward the appliquéd strip.

3. With right sides together, pin and sew the chocolate strips to the top and bottom of the quilt center. Press the seam allowances toward the strips.

FINISHING THE QUILT

Visit ShopMartingale.com/HowtoQuilt to download free illustrated information on finishing techniques.

1. Layer the backing, batting, and quilt top; baste.

2. Quilt as desired. Echo quilting around the leaves gives dimension and is a great filler for the open space.

3. Trim the backing and batting even with the quilt top.

4. Using the striped 3"-wide strips, make and attach binding.

5. Don't forget the label!

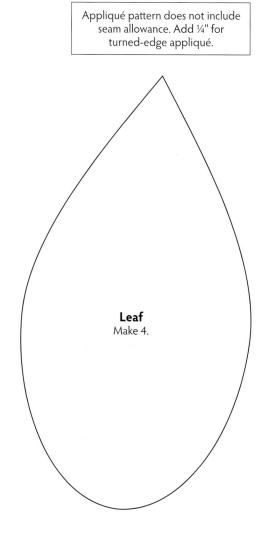

Appliqué pattern does not include seam allowance. Add ¼" for turned-edge appliqué.

Leaf
Make 4.

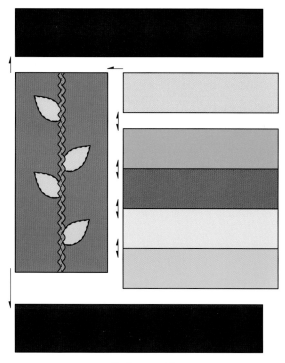

Quilt assembly

CORDUROY COBWEBS

Pieced by Stephanie Dunphy and quilted by Jane Williams

FINISHED QUILT: 54½" x 54½" ◆ FINISHED BLOCK: 9" x 9"

String quilts are easy, mindless, fun, and addictive. Making the blocks is like eating potato chips—once you start, you can't stop. Here is a fun way to use up your leftover corduroy.

I've paired my leftover corduroy from this book's projects with cotton Halloween fabric to make a "spooktacular" quilt. The strings are constructed on a muslin foundation, so I often omit the batting and use a cozy backing such as flannel or corduroy. You don't have to use muslin for the foundation; any cotton fabric will work. Use up what you have.

MATERIALS

Yardage is based on 42"-wide fabric.

4½ yards *total* of Halloween-print cottons and assorted corduroys for blocks
2⅞ yards of muslin for block foundations
⅝ yard of black print cotton for binding
3½ yards of fabric for backing
60" x 60" piece of batting (optional)

Fabric Selection
My leftover corduroy includes black-and-white houndstooth, black-and-white polka-dot, orange, limeade, kiwi, Kelly green, gray, and black.

CUTTING

From the Halloween-print cottons and assorted corduroys, cut a *total* of:*
350 to 400 strips, 1" to 2½" wide x 4" to 15" long
The exact number of strips required will depend on the width of the strips used in each block. Longer strips are perfectly fine, since you'll randomly cut the strip lengths as you sew. Throw your strips in a basket and have them ready to grab and sew.

From the muslin, cut:
9 strips, 10" x 42"; cut into 36 squares, 10" x 10"

From the black print cotton, cut:
6 strips, 3" x 42"

Change It Up
Adjusting the size of your block is as simple as changing the size of your muslin foundation square. This is the best scrap-busting project ever. However, it also makes great theme quilts, whether Christmas, patriotic, or polka dot. Have you got a lot of blue scraps? How about making a "Stringing the Blues" quilt? The possibilities are endless.

MAKING THE BLOCKS

1. Lay one print strip diagonally across the center of a muslin square, right side facing up. The placement doesn't have to be exact; just make sure the strip extends beyond the edges of the muslin square after it's flipped open and pressed. With right sides together, place a second print strip on top of the center strip with the raw edges aligned. Sew along the long edges. Flip the strip open and press.

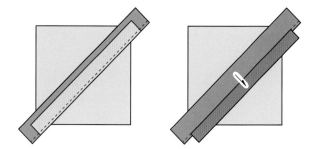

2. Continue adding strips in the same way until one corner of the muslin square is completely covered.

3. Rotate the muslin square 180°. Sew strips on the opposite corner of the square in the same manner as before until the entire muslin square is covered.

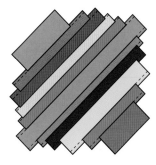

Make 36.

4. Place the block on a cutting mat with the muslin square facing up. Center a 9½" square ruler on the muslin square. Using a rotary cutter, trim the first two sides of the block. Turn the block around and cut the other two sides.

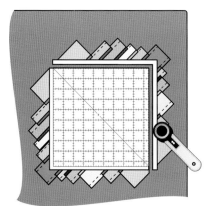

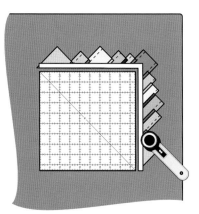

5. Repeat to make a total of 36 blocks.

Make 36.

ASSEMBLING THE QUILT TOP

1. Arrange the blocks in six rows of six blocks each as shown in the quilt assembly diagram, or experiment with different layouts if you prefer.

2. When you are pleased with the arrangement, sew the blocks together into rows, using a ¼" seam allowance. Press the seam allowances open.

3. Join the rows, matching the seam intersections. Press the seam allowances open.

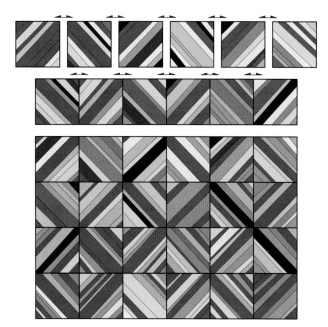

Quilt assembly

FINISHING THE QUILT

Visit ShopMartingale.com/HowtoQuilt to download free illustrated information on finishing techniques.

1. Layer the backing, batting (if desired), and quilt top; baste. It is perfectly fine to omit the batting, if you wish, since the muslin adds an extra layer of fabric.

2. Quilt as desired.

3. Trim the backing and batting even with the quilt top.

4. Using the black 3"-wide strips, make and attach binding.

5. Don't forget the label!

PLENTY OF RAINDROPS

Pieced by Stephanie Dunphy and quilted by Jane Williams

FINISHED QUILT: 48½" x 48½" ◆ FINISHED BLOCK: 4" x 4"

MATERIALS

Yardage is based on 42"-wide fabric.

1½ yards of lime solid corduroy for blocks
1⅜ yards *total* of assorted print cottons for blocks
⅝ yard of green cotton for binding
3¼ yards of fabric for backing
54" x 54" piece of batting

CUTTING

From the lime solid corduroy, cut:
5 strips, 4½" x 42"; cut into 36 squares, 4½" x 4½"
5 strips, 5" x 42"; cut into 36 squares, 5" x 5"

From the assorted print cottons, cut a *total* of:
72 squares, 5" x 5"

From the green cotton, cut:
6 strips, 3" x 42"

The original version of this quilt is called "Sparkle Plenty," using bright polka dots paired with black-and-white polka dots. When I needed a new name to reflect the adorable rainy-day fabric used in this corduroy remake, my daughter, Allison, solved my dilemma instantly. Perhaps she identifies with raindrops from her years of living in Oregon.

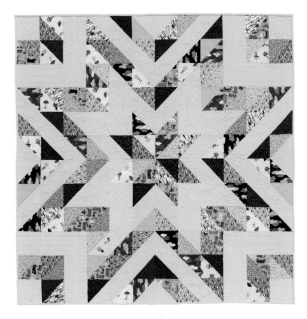

ASSEMBLING THE QUILT TOP

1. Lay out the blocks and lime 4½" squares in six rows, making sure the blocks are oriented as shown. Pin and sew the pieces together into rows. Press the seam allowances in opposite directions from row to row. Pin and sew the rows together, matching the seam intersections. Press the seam allowances open. Make four large blocks.

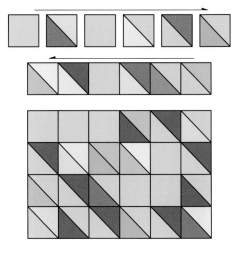

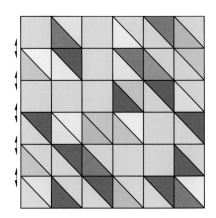

Make 4.

MAKING THE BLOCKS

1. Select 36 of the print squares. Layer a print square right sides together with a lime 5" square. Draw a diagonal line from corner to corner on the wrong side of the lighter square. Sew ¼" from the drawn line on both sides. Using a ruler and a rotary cutter, cut the squares apart on the drawn line. Press the seam allowances toward the darker fabric. Trim the blocks to measure 4½" square. Make a total of 72 triangle blocks.

Make 72.

2. Repeat step 1 using the remaining print squares to make 36 triangle blocks.

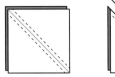

Make 36.

2. On a design wall, arrange the large blocks in two rows of two blocks each, making sure a star pattern radiates from the center outward to each corner. When you are satisfied with the arrangement, pin and sew the blocks together into rows, matching the seam intersections. Press the seam allowances open. Pin and sew the rows together. Press the seam allowances open.

Quilt assembly

FINISHING THE QUILT

Visit ShopMartingale.com/HowtoQuilt to download free illustrated information on finishing techniques.

1. Layer the backing, batting, and quilt top; baste.
2. Quilt as desired.
3. Trim the backing and batting even with the quilt top.
4. Using the green 3"-wide strips, make and attach binding.
5. Don't forget the label!

SALTWATER TAFFY

Designed by Allison Dunphy, pieced by Stephanie Dunphy, and quilted by Jackie Kunkel

FINISHED QUILT: 59¾" x 59¾" • FINISHED BLOCK: 8¼" x 8¼"

Happiness is a daughter with an eye for color and pattern. One year when Allison saw my kaleidoscope coloring page on the table, she asked if she could color it. Yes, please. In no time a lovely design appeared in shades of blue and yellow. I pieced the quilt based on her design and it became my nephew's wedding quilt. When I wanted to re-create the same pattern in corduroy, Allison suggested the color placement for the design from the color palette I planned. With these colors, the first thing we thought of was saltwater taffy. Yum! A design sheet is provided to help you create your own kaleidoscope beauty.

MATERIALS

Yardage is based on 42"-wide fabric.

3½ yards of blue solid corduroy for blocks, inner and outer borders, and binding
1 yard of tan solid corduroy for blocks
1 yard of orange solid corduroy for blocks
⅞ yard of lime solid corduroy for blocks and middle border*
3⅞ yards of fabric for backing*
65" x 65" piece of batting
Template plastic or thin cardboard

*If you prefer to cut the middle border from the lengthwise grain, you'll need 2 yards of lime solid. If you want to use corduroy for the quilt back, you'll need 4½ yards of lime solid and you can omit the backing yardage.

CUTTING

From the lime solid corduroy, cut:
2 strips, 5" x 42"
2 strips, 4" x 42"; crosscut into 12 squares, 4" x 4". Cut each square in half diagonally to yield 24 triangles.
6 strips, 1½" x 42"

From the *crosswise grain* of the blue solid corduroy, cut:
4 strips, 5" x 42"
2 strips, 4" x 42"; crosscut into 16 squares, 4" x 4". Cut each square in half diagonally to yield 32 triangles.
7 strips, 3" x 42"

From the *lengthwise grain* of the blue solid corduroy, cut:
2 strips, 4½" x 44"
2 strips, 4½" x 52"
2 strips, 4½" x 54"
2 strips, 4½" x 64"

Continued on page 84

Continued from page 83

From the tan solid corduroy, cut:

4 strips, 5" x 42"

2 strips, 4" x 42"; crosscut into 16 squares, 4" x 4".
Cut each square in half diagonally to yield
32 triangles.

From the orange solid corduroy, cut:

5 strips, 5" x 42"

1 strip, 4" x 42"; crosscut into 6 squares, 4" x 4".
Cut each square in half diagonally to yield
12 triangles.

1. Using template plastic or thin cardboard, make a template of the wedge pattern on page 87.

2. Trace the template onto the right side of a 5"-wide strip, aligning the template with the raw edge of the strip and rotating the template as shown. The drawn lines are the cutting lines.

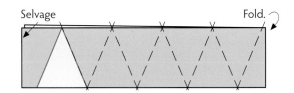

3. Lay a ruler along the drawn lines and cut along each line. If your strip is folded with the selvages aligned, you can cut two wedges at once, saving time. Cut 60 tan wedges, 52 blue wedges, 24 lime wedges, and 64 orange wedges.

Helpful Tips

- *Make a practice block first. (I like to do this with all my projects.)*

- *Cut all of your wedges and half squares, and then stack them by color and keep them on a tray near your sewing machine.*

- *Labeling each block with a scrap of paper pinned to the top edge will help keep the layout orderly.*

- *Enlarging the quilt assembly diagram is helpful if you like a bigger target!*

- *If you use a design wall, pin each block to the wall. Tragedy can strike in the form of a sneeze, vacuum, or enthusiastic children or critters. Better to be safe than sorry.*

- *Leaving the scrap of paper or small pin in the top of each block during block assembly will save lots of frustration if you accidentally turn the blocks. Just remember that the pin always signifies the top of the block.*

4. To make block A, lay out seven tan wedges and one blue wedge as shown. Pin and sew the wedges together into pairs. Press the seam allowances open and trim the little ears even with the edge of the wedge. Join the pairs to make two half blocks; press. Pin and sew the two halves together, matching the seam intersection. Press the seam allowances open.

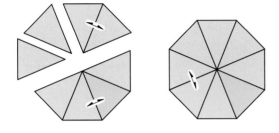

5. Fold two tan triangles and two lime triangles in half and finger-press to mark the center of the long side. Fold the block unit diagonally in half and finger-press to mark centering lines as shown. With right sides together, sew tan triangles to opposite sides of the block, matching the center creases. Sew lime triangles to the block in the same way. Flip the triangles open and press the seam allowances open. The triangles will be oversized.

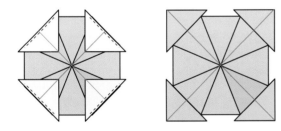

6. Using a square ruler, trim the triangles even with the edges of the block. The Kaleidoscope block should measure 8¾" square. Repeat to make a total of four of block A.

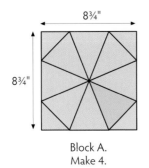

8¾"

8¾"

Block A.
Make 4.

7. Repeat steps 1–4 to make eight of block B, four of block C, four of block D, four of block E, and one of block F.

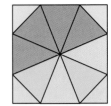

Block B.
Make 8.

Block C.
Make 4.

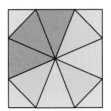

Block D.
Make 4.

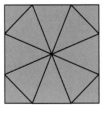

Block E.
Make 4.

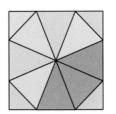

Block F.
Make 1.

ASSEMBLING THE QUILT TOP

1. On a design wall or other flat surface, lay out the blocks in five rows of five blocks each, rotating the blocks as shown in the quilt assembly diagram. Pin and sew the blocks together into rows, matching the seam intersections. Press the seam allowances open.

2. Pin and sew the rows together, matching the seam intersections. Press the seam allowances open. The quilt center should measure 41¾" x 41¾".

3. To add the inner border, pin and sew blue 44"-long strips to opposite sides of the quilt center. Press the seam allowances toward the strips. Trim the ends even with the quilt edges. Pin and sew blue 52"-long strips to the top and bottom of the quilt center to complete the inner border. Press the seam allowances toward the border strips and trim the ends even with the quilt edges.

4. Join the lime 1½"-wide strips end to end. From the pieced strip, cut four 54"-long strips. Repeat step 3 to add the lime strips to the quilt top for the middle border.

5. Repeat step 3 to sew the blue 54"-long strips to the sides of the quilt. Press and trim. Then sew the blue 64"-long strips to the top and bottom of the quilt to complete the outer border. Press and trim.

FINISHING THE QUILT

Visit ShopMartingale.com/HowtoQuilt to download free illustrated information on finishing techniques.

1. Layer the backing, batting, and quilt top; baste.

2. Quilt as desired.

3. Trim the backing and batting even with the quilt top.

4. Using the blue 3"-wide strips, make and attach binding.

5. Don't forget your label!

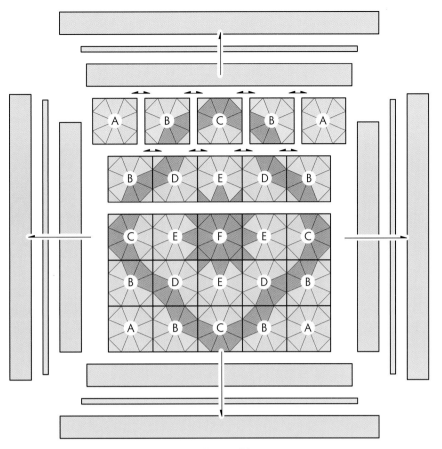

Quilt assembly

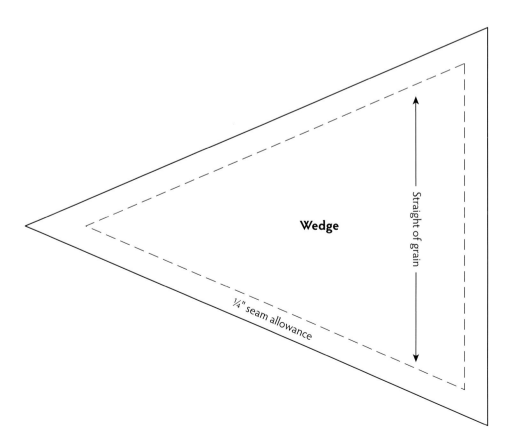

Wedge

Straight of grain

¼" seam allowance

Design sheet

The poppy is the state flower of California, where I grew up in the 1960s and '70s. Today I'm a California girl living in a Midwestern world, but this wall hanging is reminiscent of fields of poppies and the burnt oranges and avocado greens of my childhood era. Peace, love, and poppies.

CALIFORNIA POPPIES

Pieced by Stephanie Dunphy and quilted by Jane Williams

FINISHED QUILT: 24½" x 42" ◆ FINISHED BLOCK: 8" x 38"

MATERIALS

Yardage is based on 42"-wide fabric.

1 yard of cream corduroy for background
⅝ yard of green dotted cotton for leaves, rectangles, and binding
¼ yard *total* of assorted orange print cottons for flowers
¼ yard of green print cotton for leaves
¼ yard of green striped cotton for stems
⅛ yard of orange striped cotton for stem
6 scraps, 4" x 4", of assorted floral cottons for circle appliqués
1½ yards of fabric for backing
30" x 48" piece of batting
1 yard of ⅜"-wide orange rickrack
9 small, very cute buttons
Template plastic or thin cardboard
Seam sealant

CUTTING

From the cream corduroy, cut:
1 strip, 4½" x 42"; cut into 3 rectangles, 4½" x 8½"
4 strips, 3¾" x 42"; cut into:
   6 rectangles, 3¾" x 16"
   6 rectangles, 3¾" x 5"
   6 rectangles, 2" x 3¾"
1 strip, 3½" x 42"; cut into 6 squares, 3½" x 3½"
2 strips, 2½" x 42"; cut into 24 squares, 2½" x 2½"

From the assorted orange print cottons, cut a *total* of:
3 rectangles, 6½" x 8½"

From the green print cotton, cut:
8 squares, 3¾" x 3¾"

From the green dotted cotton, cut:
4 squares, 3¾" x 3¾"
3 rectangles, 4" x 8½"
4 strips, 3" x 42"

Continued on page 91

Continued from page 89

From the green striped cotton, cut:
2 strips, 2" x 28½"

From the orange striped cotton, cut:
1 strip, 2" x 28½"

From the orange rickrack, cut:
9 pieces, 3½" long

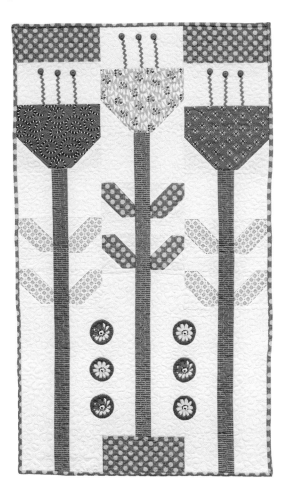

MAKING THE POPPY BLOCKS

1. Referring to "Making Folded Corners" on page 11, use the orange 6½" x 8½" rectangles and cream 3½" squares to make three flower units as shown. The units should measure 6½" x 8½".

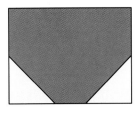

Make 3.

2. In the same manner, use the green 3¾" squares and cream 2½" squares to make 12 leaf units as shown.

Make 12.

3. On each cream 4½" x 8½" rectangle, lightly mark a center line. Then mark lines 2½" in from each short end, stopping each line 1" from the top edge.

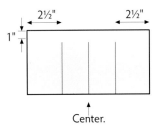

Center.

4. Center a piece of rickrack on top of each drawn line. Pin in place and sew through the center of the rickrack. Trim the bottom tails even with the edge of the rectangle. Use a dab of seam sealant at the top ends of the rickrack to prevent fraying. Make three units.

5. Lay out one rickrack unit from step 4, one flower unit from step 1, four leaf units from step 2, one green or orange striped strip, two cream 3¾" x 5" rectangles, two cream 2" x 3¾" rectangles, and two cream 3¾" x 16" rectangles as shown. Pin and sew the pieces into rows. Press the seam allowances in the directions indicated. Join the rows to complete the block and press. Make a total of three Poppy blocks.

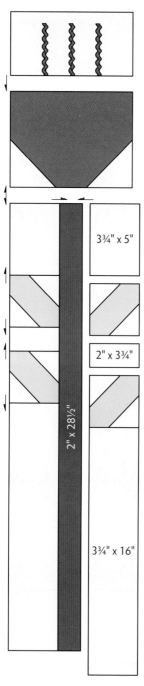

3¾" x 5"

2" x 3¾"

2" x 28½"

3¾" x 16"

Make 3.

ASSEMBLING THE QUILT TOP

1. Lay out the Poppy blocks and green dotted rectangles as shown in the quilt assembly diagram below. Pin and sew the pieces together into vertical rows. Press the seam allowances toward the green rectangles. Join the rows and press the seam allowances open.

2. Using heat-resistant template plastic or thin cardboard, make a template of the circle pattern on page 93. Lightly trace a circle onto the wrong side of each floral square. Cut out the circles, adding a ¼" seam allowance. Thread a needle and knot one end. Sew a running stitch close to the outer raw edge of the circle. Place the template in the center of the fabric circle, and pull the thread to gather the seam allowance over the template. Press the edges on the front and back of the circle. Carefully remove the template and gently pull the thread to adjust the circle, if needed. Press the circle again. Make six circle appliqués.

3. Pin three circles on each seam line, making sure they are evenly spaced and centered on the seams as shown. Appliqué in place using your desired method.

Quilt assembly

CALIFORNIA POPPIES

FINISHING THE QUILT

Visit ShopMartingale.com/HowtoQuilt to download free illustrated information on finishing techniques.

1. Layer the backing, batting, and quilt top; baste.
2. Quilt as desired.
3. Trim the backing and batting even with the quilt top.
4. Using the green dotted 3"-wide strips, make and attach binding.
5. Center a button at the top of each rickrack segment, making sure to cover the ends, and sew in place.
6. Make a hanging sleeve, if desired. Don't forget your label!

> Appliqué pattern does not include seam allowance. Add ¼" for turned-edge appliqué.

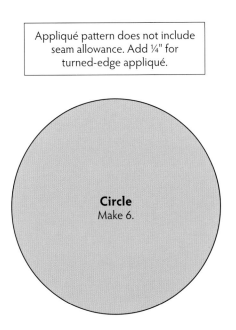

Circle
Make 6.

RESOURCES

I encourage you to support your local quilt shops. The following sites are resources for supplies if you can't find what you need locally.

CORDUROY MANUFACTURERS

FreeSpirit
FreeSpiritFabric.com

Robert Kaufman Fabrics
RobertKaufman.com

Westminster Fabrics
WestminsterFabrics.com

ONLINE CORDUROY SOURCES

Beverly's
Beverlys.com

Fabric Depot
FabricDepot.com

Fabric.com
Fabric.com

OTHER FABRICS AND NOTIONS

ByAnnie
ByAnnie.com
Soft and Stable

Connecting Threads
ConnectingThreads.com
Fabric and thread

Hobby Lobby
HobbyLobby.com
Corduroy fabric, batting, and bag-making supplies

JoAnn Fabrics
JoAnn.com
Corduroy fabric, batting, and bag-making supplies

Michael Miller Fabrics Inc.
MichaelMillerFabrics.com
Fabric

The Ribbon Jar
RibbonJar.com
Ribbons, trims, and rickrack

United Notions
UnitedNotions.com
Fabric

LONG-ARM QUILTING SERVICES

Jane Williams of **A Lady in Thread**
jane@aladyinthread.com

Linda Hrcka of **The Quilted Pineapple**
TheQuiltedPineapple.com

ACKNOWLEDGMENTS

Family first, always. I am thankful for:

* Dave, my husband—for knowing when I need flowers and for being the best mister ever!

* Allison—daughter extraordinaire, for her design talents, fabulous color sense, and computer skills.

* James, my son—for his quirky sense of humor and for unknowingly giving me the idea for the book.

* Gladys Knight had her Pips, Diana Ross had the Supremes, but I have my own fabulous backup team that's second to none. They are the best pattern testers ever. I am grateful for their time, talent, generosity, support, patience, and enthusiasm. Although each project in this book is made by me, each one was also tested for accuracy. The following ladies are members of the choir and they sing beautifully: Simone de Klerk (The Netherlands), Margaret Goodson (Spain), Mary Kolb, Carol Lewis, Sherri McConnell, Nonnie Meelia, Candace Pekich, Carrie Pippins, Marumi Prince, Mary Schuberg, and Charmaine Taylor (all from the United States), and Ulla Rantakari (Finland).

Amazingly creative long-arm quilters who worked their magic on my quilts—Jackie Kunkel of Canton Village Quilt Works, Jane Williams of A Lady in Thread, and Linda Hrcka of The Quilted Pineapple.

Connecting Threads—Anita McIntire and Alisha Runckel generously provided fabric and thread, as well as support and encouragement.

Karen Burns at Martingale—for understanding the importance of polka dots.

ABOUT THE AUTHOR

After my two less-than-stellar attempts at home economics in 7th and 9th grades, my talented mom probably feared that the creative gene had skipped a generation. I preferred playing softball and running track.

My sister and I always groaned when Mom took us on those dreaded trips to the fabric store for "just a minute." To a 10-year-old that always seemed like hours. I'm certain that's where my fascination with buttons began, as I sat impatiently yet mesmerized by the wall of buttons in all colors, shapes, and sizes.

Fast-forward to the early 1990s and I'm married with two small children, living in Japan and needing Halloween costumes. I finally learned to sew, but mostly because of my newfound love for quilting. I learned the sewing basics and then took the first quilting class offered at the military base's recreation center.

A decade later I'm living in Pickerington, Ohio; my kids are in college; and I've learned about Etsy and blogs from my daughter. With her encouragement and help, I set up Loft Creations and started selling handmade items. When I started my blog, I wondered if anyone would visit or if I would just talk amongst myself! I'm happy to say I've been found.

My style is an eclectic mix, and I'm a proud lover of buttons, polka dots, and *all* things tea. I'm lucky to have the support of my family and friends. Happiness is sipping tea and sewing with my dear Abby by my side. Through my sewing journey I have learned that *handmade is best!*

To learn more about me, please visit my Loft Creations website at designsbyloftcreations.com. You'll find more patterns, tutorials, and plenty of inspiration.

Top: the Scooter Bug children (and Abby, the faithful dog);
bottom: Dad and his Ford Fairlane.